**If you don't claim it, you don't get it.
That's money down the drain
for millions of Americans.**

—Mark Everson, Former IRS Commissioner

Write It Off! Deduct It!

The A-to-Z Guide to Tax Deductions for Home-Based Businesses

Bernard B. Kamoroff, CPA

TAYLOR TRADE PUBLISHING
Lanham • Boulder • New York • London

Published by Taylor Trade Publishing
An imprint of The Rowman & Littlefield Publishing Group, Inc.
4501 Forbes Boulevard, Suite 200, Lanham, Maryland 20706
www.rowman.com

Unit A, Whitacre Mews, 26-34 Stannary Street, London SE11 4AB, United Kingdom

Distributed by NATIONAL BOOK NETWORK

British Library Cataloguing in Publication Information Available

Library of Congress Cataloging-in-Publication Data
Kamoroff, Bernard, author.
    Write it off! deduct it! : the A-to-Z guide to tax deductions for home-based businesses / Bernard B. Kamoroff.
    pages cm
    ISBN 978-1-63076-069-4 (pbk. : alk. paper) — ISBN 978-1-63076-070-0 (electronic)
    1. Income tax deductions for home office expenses—United States. 2. Home-based businesses—Taxation—Law and legislation—United States. I. Title.
    KF6395.B88K36 2015
    343.7305'23—dc23
                                                                        2014039783

∞ ™ The paper used in this publication meets the minimum requirements of American National Standard for Information Sciences—Permanence of Paper for Printed Library Materials, ANSI/NISO Z39.48-1992.

Printed in the United States of America

Please Read

I have done my very best to give you useful and accurate information in this book, but I cannot guarantee that the information is correct or will be appropriate to your particular situation. Laws and regulations change frequently and are subject to differing interpretations. It is your responsibility to verify all information and all laws discussed in this book before relying on them. Nothing in this book can substitute for legal advice and cannot be considered as making it unnecessary to obtain such advice. Obtain specific information from the Internal Revenue Service or a competent person.

Give me a list of write-offs organized by type of deduction, and you're guaranteed to knock half off your tax preparation bill.

—Andrew Blackman, CPA, New York City

Contents

Preface:
A Treasure Hunt

Every home-based business owner is looking for ways to reduce expenses without cutting corners, reducing quality, or losing customers. But few businesses look to the one area almost guaranteed to save you money: your tax return.

Last year, America's small businesses overpaid their income taxes by more than $2 billion, according to a CPA study reported in *Business 2000 Magazine*. The overpayments were made because the businesses failed to take tax deductions they were legally entitled to take. Many of these businesses are still unaware of their errors. They overpaid their taxes and don't even know it.

The IRS is not going to help these businesses. The IRS will never tell you about a tax deduction you didn't claim. That's up to you.

Whether you struggle with your own tax return, hire an accountant, or put your trust in a software program, the more you know about what's deductible, the more you'll save on your taxes. Your tax return lists only a handful of deductions, so it is up to you to make sure you find and claim every one. It really is a treasure hunt.

Every tax deduction you find in this book will reduce your taxes, honestly, legitimately, and with the full approval and blessings of the Internal Revenue Service.

It is very much like finding free money.

A tax is a compulsory payment for which no specific benefit is received.

—U.S. Treasury

It is our Patriotic Duty to keep as much money out of the hands of our government as we can.

—Walter Camp, philosopher

Introduction: The Home-Based Business

I'd guess that on every city block and on every rural road in the United States, someone is operating a business out of a home. The U.S. Bureau of Labor Statistics and the Small Business Administration report that there are more than nineteen million home-based businesses in the United States—56 percent of all businesses in the United States—and they generate $102 billion in annual revenue.

What Is a "Home" Business?

The term "home business" (or "home-based business") applies to anyone working for himself or herself, whose main business location is in the home or in a separate structure on the home property. "Home business" also applies to self-employed individuals who earn their income away from home, such as contractors and tradespeople, but who do their business administrative work (scheduling, paying bills, posting their records, etc.) at a home office.

The term "home business" applies not just to businesses that buy and sell goods, but to home-based inventors, contractors, professionals, freelancers, designers, consultants, Internet entrepreneurs, anyone who is self-employed and working from home.

Home Business and the IRS

As far as the IRS is concerned, a home business is no different than any other business. Home business owners file business tax returns, report earnings as business income, and deduct business expenses. What *is* different about a home business is that not only can you deduct the business expenses that every business is entitled to, you can turn personal, nondeductible expenses into tax-deductible business expenses—if you are careful to follow the rules. The IRS has some very specific income tax laws that apply only to home-based businesses. These are all covered here.

The biggest home-business tax issue is the Home Office deduction, which has generated more confusion—and fear of the IRS—than any other business tax law. This is the deduction that allows you to write off the part of your home that is used for business. The deduction is covered thoroughly in the listings under "Home Office." I just want to emphasize here that Congress gave home businesses this deduction. It's legal, it can save you a bundle of money.

The Home Office deduction, like every business deduction, is up to you to claim. If you don't claim it, you don't get it. The IRS is not going to hand it to you, is not going to ask you why you didn't take it, in fact is not going to care at all if you don't claim a deduction and want to pay them more tax money than you have to.

I mention this in the Home Office listing, but it bears repeating: Failure to qualify for the home office deduction doesn't prohibit you from operating your business out of your home. It only means that one possibly large expense, the cost of the home office itself, is not deductible on your federal income taxes. You can still deduct all legitimate business expenses other than those directly related to the business space itself.

1

Introduction to Tax Deductions

Relax

Relax. Tax law isn't easy, but this book is.

This book will not try to explain how to prepare a tax return. This book will not have you struggling with tax forms. This book will not drag you through the confusing, contradictory, confounding world of tax law.

This book *will* let you know about hundreds of tax deductions that are available to every home-based business, self-employed individual, independent contractor: anyone working from home or with an office in the home, full time or part time.

A CPA by the name of George Brown, who was interviewed in a business magazine, made a statement that has stuck with me for several years and that inspired this book: "You get a raise every time you can legitimately avoid paying a tax on something." Every tax deduction you find will save you money on your federal income taxes, on your state income taxes, on your self-employment taxes, on local income taxes, and on any other business taxes based on net profit.

If you really like the challenge of preparing your own tax return, I encourage you to do it. And if you don't want to struggle with tax forms, leave that miserable job to your tax accountant. Either way, you owe it to yourself to find every tax deduction you can.

Who Is This Book For?

This book is for anyone working for himself or herself. This includes sole proprietors, partners in partnerships, members of limited liability companies (LLCs), and people who own their own corporations.

This book is for sales businesses, repair people, manufacturers, trades people, freelancers, professionals, independent contractors, outside contractors, subcontractors, general contractors, contract laborers, entrepreneurs, consultants, mail-order businesses, Internet businesses, artists, craftspeople, direct marketers, network marketers, multilevel marketers, free agents, virtual assistants, sales reps, inventors, moonlighters, full time, part time, sideline—you name it. Unless you are on someone else's payroll as an employee, you are in business for yourself. You are entitled to all the business deductions in this book.

This book is for anyone who gets a 1099-MISC form, the IRS's "Miscellaneous Income" form that businesses give to individuals who are doing contract work but are not on the payroll as an employee.

This book is not for employees: people on the payroll of an employer, having taxes deducted from their paychecks, getting a W-2 statement at year end. (If you are an employee/owner of your own corporation, this book is for you.)

This book is not for investors, people making money in the stock market or commodities trading, people earning their money from rental income or loans or interest or dividends, people earning what the IRS calls "passive" income. But this book is for people who manage property, rentals, commodities, etc., or offer consulting or advice or financial services related to these investments. This book is for people who invest in their own businesses, but not for people who invest in other people's businesses.

How to Use This Book to Your Best Advantage

Be forewarned. This guide does not provide complete information on all federal tax laws nor was it intended to. There are already enough publications available that do just that, and they are not easy to read either.

This guide does list every business tax deduction for home-based businesses that I have encountered in thirty years of tax practice, consulting, writing, teaching, and running my own home-based businesses. I let you know what the deductions are, and whether they apply to you and your business.

Tax laws are precise, and I've tried to make this book as precise as possible, but without making it so confusing and complicated that it becomes unreadable—like most of the tax guides on the market. I've tried to accomplish this task with a three-step system:

Step 1: For each tax deduction, I define the terminology (and not in IRS Code Sections, accountant's jargon, or other forms of advanced Sanskrit), and I explain the basic laws. These laws apply to most businesses, most of the time. "Most" is the key word. There may be exceptions.

Step 2: If there are exceptions to the laws, or complications, or special situations for some businesses, I alert you to these fun details and explain them in general, but without bogging you down in confusing or complicated tax law.

Step 3: If necessary, I refer you to one of the free IRS publications that have the fine-print details of the laws. You can then do your own research (which really isn't all that difficult if you take it one deduction at a time), or you can ask your accountant about the details. Either way, you now know that there may be yet another tax savings worth looking into.

The wording in tax law is important. The words have very specific meanings. Don't read more into the laws than what is explained here, don't read between the lines, don't make assumptions, as you can easily wind up making assumptions that are inaccurate.

Be particularly aware that terms such as "up to" and "as much as" mean that the dollar amounts shown are maximums in some circumstances and not in others. These terms usually show up in complicated laws with too many exceptions to list here.

If the terminology is confusing or unclear, if you do not understand a word, a definition, or an explanation, it is important that you stop and take the time to understand its meaning before using the information. If you don't fully understand the concepts, ask. Get help from your accountant. Misunderstanding tax law can lead to trouble.

I'd also like to give you a warning about getting help from the IRS. Although IRS publications are usually accurate and reliable, the same cannot always be said of tax information the IRS gives out over the phone or in person. The IRS people do, on occasion, give out totally incorrect information. Tax laws are vastly complicated and even the experts make mistakes. Do not rely on verbal information unless you can verify it. Ask the IRS person for a reference to one of their publications, and then look it up.

Expense Category

Every deduction listed in this book includes an expense category. The expense category is a guide to help you fill out your tax return, to figure out what line on the tax return to post each deduction.

Schedule C, the business tax return for sole proprietors, lists only 24 categories of expense: 24 line items. The partnership tax return (Form 1065), the Limited Liability Company tax return (also using Form 1065), the C corporation tax return (Form 1120), and the S corporation tax return (1120-S) list a similar numbers of categories. And here we have 475 deductions to combine into 24 categories. Where do the 475 deductions go? What categories?

Some categories are obvious. Interest goes on the "Interest" line. Advertising goes on the "Advertising" line. Pencils go on the "Office expense" line. But where do you stick Education expenses? Freight? Decorating expenses? Alarm systems? You can use the "Expense category" designations in the book as a guide.

Keep in mind that these expense categories are only a guide. They are not law, not rigid. It is not critical which deductions go on which lines on the tax form. The IRS is not going to be upset if an expense that belongs on one line winds up on another. Even I'm not sure whether some deductions should be labeled "Office expense" or "Supplies" or something else. If you have a deduction you don't know where to put on the tax return, just pick a reasonable category and put it there.

It is a good idea to make a worksheet showing which expenses you combined for the tax return, and keep it with your copy of your return (no need to send it to the IRS). This will make things a lot easier should you ever face an audit, or if you need to check your figures later, or if you are just looking back a year later trying to figure out how to fill out the next year's tax return.

There is a line on the tax return called "Other expenses," used for deductions that don't fit into any other category. Many of the deductions in this book are shown as "Other expenses," because there really is no appropriate category on the tax return. But remember that the category you pick is not critical. What is critical is that you take every deduction you are entitled to, regardless of where you put it on the tax return.

Deductions you do include as part of "Other expenses" should be listed individually. The tax return provides a separate area for listing the deductions that comprise "Other expenses." List each expense separately, then show the total on the "Other expenses" line on the return.

Is Every Possible Tax Deduction Listed?

This list of 475 deductions is compiled from my studies of tax laws for more than thirty years (somebody's got to do it, right?), my background as a CPA, my experience working directly with hundreds of different businesses of all types, and the generous feedback I've gotten from my readers and people who attend my seminars.

But still, I'd be a fool to say that I've listed every possible deduction there is. If you have a deduction not listed in this book, and if it meets the basic rules for all deductions (covered below), by all means take it. Or at least ask your accountant about it. And let me know about it too, will you? Maybe the next edition of this book will have *476* tax deductions.

Isn't This What You Pay Your Accountant For?

Here is the most important piece of information in this book: You have to find these deductions yourself. Only you know the ins and outs of your own business. You cannot rely 100 percent on your bookkeeper, your accountant, your attorney, your software program, or the Internal Revenue Service.

Any experienced tax accountant will (or certainly should) know about every tax deduction listed in this book. But your accountant can't possibly take the time to ask you about every possible deduction you didn't know about or failed to include on your ledgers. The typical tax accountant may have several hundred tax clients, and during the three hectic months of "tax season" (January 15 to April 15), your accountant is preparing a dozen or maybe two dozen tax returns a day. The accountant most likely wants to take your year's totals, totals you yourself have summarized from your records, enter them into the computer, push "Print," and collect his $250. Next.

If you are expecting an accountant to actually sit down with you, discuss tax deductions in detail, study your business and your records, and find you savings, you should plan to do this well before the tax preparation time, and expect to pay about $100 an hour for this service. And even then, you really should not expect an accountant who does not work day to day in your business to be able to rattle off every possible tax deduction you may be entitled to.

Instead, spend a few hours with this book. Skim the alphabetical list of deductions, and spot the ones that may apply to you. And then, if needed, ask your accountant about them. Your accountant will be of much greater help, and much greater value, if you first go through these 475 deductions before seeing the accountant. By doing a little homework, you may significantly reduce the accounting fees.

The well-known tax attorney Julian Block said it best: "The informed client gets the best advice."

Will Your Deductions Trigger an Audit?

Are you afraid to take certain deductions because you fear they may trigger an audit? Welcome to the club. There are thousands of small business people paying millions of dollars in taxes they don't owe, year after year, simply out of fear of being audited.

"Don't take the home office deduction, it'll guarantee an audit." What home-business owner hasn't heard that? It is a myth. The home office deduction does not invite an audit. And the same applies to most tax deductions.

But, yes, there are a few tax deductions that are red flags, ones likely to bounce your return out of the computer and put that nasty gleam in the eye of some IRS auditor, deductions that are likely to invite an audit, and, again yes, ones you may want to avoid—or at least be careful about—when preparing your tax return.

Those few deductions that are likely to invite an audit are mentioned in this book. They include: Large travel and entertainment deductions, probably the most likely to generate suspicion. Deductions for expenses not typically associated with your type of business. Deductions for items of a personal or recreational nature. Any large deductions out of line with the amount of income you are reporting. (Although a home office deduction does not trigger an audit, a *large* home office deduction combined with a small income does increase your chances of being audited.)

What *will* increase your odds of being audited are not so much the deductions, but other things on your tax return: A loss year after year, especially for people who also have earnings from a job. An occupation targeted by the IRS because of potential "abuse" (ease of cheating), particularly businesses that deal in cash such as self-service laundries, car washes, cab drivers, hair salons. Barter transactions. Failing to report income that was reported to the IRS on a W-2 or a 1099 Miscellaneous Income form. Non-business items that are incorrect or out of line. Claiming your dog as a dependent. Telling the IRS that the income tax is unconstitutional.

If you discover from reading this book that you have a tax deduction that may cause you trouble, it is then up to you to decide how "aggressive" you want to be, or how safe you want to be, when claiming the tax deduction. I think this book will help you make those decisions. But I recommend you talk to your tax accountant about your concerns. Any good accountant should be able to help you stay within your comfort zone.

I think that is the real key: your comfort. No amount of money is worth destroying your peace of mind. No tax savings is worth high blood pressure. But short of a sleepless night of IRS worries, if you are entitled to a tax deduction, take it. The laws were written to allow these deductions. Congress and the IRS say, "Yes, take the deductions, you don't owe the tax." If the government in its wisdom is allowing a deduction, you in your wisdom should take it.

When in Doubt, Deduct

Even after all the studying, talking to experts, and getting deep into the Internal Revenue Code, sometimes you still cannot be positive that a certain deduction is or isn't legitimate. The IRS says one thing, the Tax Court says the exact opposite, and your congressperson (who dreamed up the law) is still on vacation. What do you do?

The answer depends on your own personality, how comfortable or uncomfortable you are if you have to face an audit, and how much is at stake. If you are only going to save a few bucks but might get a Dear Taxpayer letter from the IRS, and maybe open up a Pandora's box you'd rather stay closed, it's probably not worth the risk.

But if you have nothing to hide and lots to save, I personally would go for it. Your chance of being audited, no matter what you deduct, is less than 2 percent. If you do get audited, the worst that can happen is the IRS will say "no dice," and demand the back taxes you'd owe anyway, and interest. There is usually no penalty for making an honest mistake or a reasonable interpretation of the law.

I want to make one thing clear throughout this book: If any deduction is questionable, if there is any doubt, any disagreement, any IRS opposition, I spell that out in the description of the deduction. You will not be caught by surprise; you will not have to wonder if a certain deduction can lead to possible trouble.

Tax Loopholes and Tax Secrets

Tax laws are often carelessly written. Every time a new tax law comes out, clever accountants and eagle-eyed lawyers find holes in the laws, find unintended deductions, find ways around the laws neither Congress nor the IRS intended: tax "loopholes."

Some of these tax loopholes are actually quite legitimate, but some are not, and some are what we call "gray" or questionable areas of tax law. In this book, every tax loophole that applies to a home-based business is listed and explained, so you will know which ones are legitimate deductions, which ones are questionable, and which ones are not deductible.

Do you want to know about "tax secrets"? There are none. There are no secrets in tax law. There are, however, legitimate tax deductions that few people know about, sort of a secret I guess. Every "secret" deduction that applies to business is in this book.

What isn't in this book are "tax avoidance" schemes, "abusive" tax shelters, tax scams, or dubious deductions that will get you audited. We are not out to deceive the Internal Revenue Service or anyone else. Some of the deductions listed in this book may be "tax loopholes" or "tax secrets," but they are genuine, acceptable, IRS-approved All-American Tax Deductions. And each and every one is money in your pocket that stays in your pocket.

Federal vs. State Laws

The laws explained in this book are federal tax laws, for preparing your federal tax return. Many states have the exact same laws as the feds, and most business deductions allowed on your federal return are allowed on your state return. But that is not guaranteed. You should study the instructions that come with your state tax forms, or state tax publications, or ask your accountant. You might find additional state deductions that the IRS does not allow, and save even more money on your state taxes.

"I Wish I Had This Book Last Year"
(Amending Prior Years' Tax Returns)

Did you miss some deductions on last year's tax return that you were entitled to? Well, as some newspaperman said many years ago, "Yes, Virginia, there is a Santa Claus."

You can go back and amend prior tax returns and claim a refund of prior years' taxes. Amended tax returns must be filed within three years from the date you filed your original return or within two years from the time you paid your tax, whichever is later. A return filed early is considered filed on the due date. So for 2014 tax returns filed and paid on time (April 15, 2015) or ahead of time, you have until April 15, 2018, to amend the return.

Tax returns are amended on form 1040-X for sole proprietorships, 1120-X for regular corporations, 1120-S (marked "Amended") for S corporations, and 1065 (marked "Amended") for partnerships and Limited Liability Companies. Refunds are fairly prompt.

Amended returns are not more likely to be audited than original returns.

If your federal return was in error, your state return was probably also in error. States have similar procedures for amending returns.

Keeping Records

Many legitimate tax deductions are lost because people don't know about them. That's the reason for this book. But many more tax deductions are lost simply because people failed to record them. People who do not keep good records cheat themselves out of deductions because they didn't write them down. Recordkeeping is, in fact, the very heart of taking advantage of tax deductions.

If you don't have a good set of business records, STOP. If you do not have a good system for recording every business expense, STOP. Get a set of ledgers or get an accounting software program and learn how to use it. Hire an accountant or a bookkeeper, if necessary, to help you set up the ledgers and teach you the basics. Or read my book *Small Time Operator: How to Start Your Own Business, Keep Your Books, Pay Your Taxes, and Stay Out of Trouble.*

Get receipts for everything you possibly can, set up a good filing system for the receipts, and keep the receipts at least three years. Three years from the date you file your tax return is the IRS statute of limitations for most audits. Receipts are your best proof if the IRS ever challenges a deduction. If you don't have receipts, make notes about expenses, or keep a business diary. Record mileage. And don't forget all those tiny out-of-pocket expenses; even small purchases can add up to a significant tax deduction.

The IRS says that business records can be kept on paper or stored electronically on disk or on your computer or on a service provider's website, as long as the information can be retrieved if the IRS requests it.

When Can You Take a Deduction?

Most deductions are taken the year you incur the expense. But there are many exceptions to this rule. Some prepaid expenses are deducted the year they apply to, regardless of when they are paid. Some expenses must be depreciated, which means they are written off over several years. Inventory (goods for sale) cannot be written off until the inventory is sold. In the list of 475 deductions, any expense that cannot be deducted currently is explained. You will not have to guess if an expense is currently deductible.

Cash Method vs. Accrual Accounting

You should also understand the two accounting methods allowed by the IRS: the cash method and the accrual method.

The cash method does not mean that all your transactions are in cash. It refers to how you record your purchases, and what you can deduct on this year's tax return. Under the cash method (also called "cash basis"), expenses are recorded when paid, with some exceptions. Purchases you haven't yet paid are not deducted on your tax return until paid.

Under the accrual method, all expenses are recorded whether paid or not. An expense you incur this year but do not pay until next year is recorded as this year's expense and taken as a tax deduction this year, not next year when the bill is paid.

Most small businesses choose the cash method, because it is easy to understand and requires much simpler bookkeeping.

Who can use the cash method? Businesses with annual sales of $5 million or less can use either the cash method or accrual method of accounting, your choice. Above $5 million in annual sales, most businesses other than corporations can still use the cash accounting method if annual sales are $10 million or less. Corporations (other than personal service corporations) must use accrual accounting if sales exceed $5 million a year.

Every IRS law is guaranteed to have exceptions, and the cash method is, well, no exception. Certain expenses cannot be deducted when paid, even for cash method businesses. When you look up an expense item in this book, the entry will tell you if the expense cannot be deducted currently, and when it can be deducted.

The biggest and most significant expense that cannot be deducted currently is inventory. This is covered in detail under Inventory, but the general rule is that you cannot write off the cost of your inventory until you sell it.

Year-End Payments

Checks written and mailed or delivered by December 31 can be deducted the year written, even if cashed in the new year.

Bills paid electronically are deducted the year your account is debited. If a bill is paid in December but not processed by your bank until January, the expense cannot be deducted until the next year.

Expenses charged to bank credit cards (MasterCard, VISA, Discover, American Express) are deducted the year the expense is incurred, even if paid next year. This applies to both accrual and cash method businesses. But expenses on charge cards issued by individual stores, gasoline companies, etc., cannot be deducted by cash method businesses until paid. (The IRS ought to be horsewhipped for coming up with such a complicated set of laws.)

Structuring Transactions to Your Best Tax Advantage

You want to do your best to be sure every expense of your business becomes a tax deduction. Often simply the way you structure a deal, or the way you word a contract, or how you describe an expense, can mean the difference between something that is deductible and something that isn't.

Throughout the book, I try to warn you about different expenditures that can be interpreted or structured in different ways, so you'll be able to make the tax laws work for you. And it is perfectly legal. Large corporations hire $300 per hour tax attorneys to do nothing but find ways around the taxes they don't want to pay. You get to buy this book. But don't be afraid to quiz your tax accountant about any expense that may want a little "reworking."

How many times have you heard about some business that is losing money or making a worthless purchase or spending frivolously, but, hey, it's a tax write-off. After thirty years of dealing with tax laws, I still don't find logic in this strategy. The concept of incurring an expense solely as a tax write-off is, when you get right down to it, ridiculous. The expense will always be greater than the tax write-off the expense brings, that must be obvious. (A tax "write-off" and a tax "deduction" are the same thing.)

Business transactions should not solely be tax motivated. Make sure the deal has a real economic purpose independent of tax consequences. Then figure out how to structure the deal to your best tax advantage.

Timing Transactions to Your Best Tax Advantage

As the end of the year approaches, you can structure your business transactions to increase or decrease your profit, and therefore increase or decrease the taxes you will pay. Within limits, you can postpone or accelerate purchases and other business expenses.

For example, if you are thinking of buying a new computer, you can buy it in December for a deduction this year, or buy it in January for a deduction next year. You can do same with other office equipment, supplies, repairs, etc.

If you are on the cash method of accounting, you can prepay some of next year's expenses and get a deduction this year instead of next year. Or you can postpone paying some of this year's bills until next year if you would rather get the deduction next year.

If you are on the accrual method, you do not have as much flexibility as businesses on the cash method, but you can still decide to make a large purchase in December instead of January, or vice versa.

If the current year is a low-income year, and if you already have enough deductions to bring your taxes down and keep your tax bracket at the minimum, you would probably benefit from postponing expenses to next year. If, on the other hand, this is a high-income year and you could use more deductions to reduce your tax burden, accelerating expenses, spending the money this year instead of next year, may be the best tax strategy.

You might want to talk to your accountant in November or early December about your options. Once it's New Year's Day, it's too late.

Equipment, Supplies, and Inventory Owned Before Going into Business

Items you owned before going into business that get used in the business (converted to business use), are eligible for some but not all of the tax deductions as items purchased specifically for business.

Assets converted to business use must be valued at your cost, or at their market value at the time the assets are first used in your business, whichever is less.

Business assets such as furniture, computer, tools, and equipment that were purchased before going into business, can be depreciated using the same depreciation schedules for similar assets. These assets, however, are not eligible for first-year write-off (as explained under "Business Assets" in the A-to-Z section).

Inventory and supplies are deducted exactly the same as inventory and supplies purchased specifically for the business.

If your business is a sole proprietorship, you simply put the items in your business, much as you put your cash in the business.

If the business is a partnership or limited liability company (LLC), you can still put the items in the business, but be careful how you and your business co-owners view the ownership of the items.

If your business is a corporation, you may have to legally transfer ownership to the corporation. This will require help from your accountant.

Paying Business Expenses

Who actually pays for a business expense—you the owner out of your personal non-business funds, or the business itself—can affect the deductibility of the expense.

If your business is a sole proprietorship (one owner, no partners, not incorporated, not an LLC), it does not matter whether you or your business pays the bills. If it is a business-related expense, your business gets the deduction. If you make business purchases on a credit card or debit card, the card does not have to be in the business name. Your business vehicle does not have to be registered in the business name, your business building does not have to be rented or purchased in the business name. You still get the deduction.

If your business is a partnership, corporation, or limited liability company, the laws are very different. Business deductions are sometimes disallowed when claimed by the business owners or employees, instead of by the companies themselves. Try not to pay business expenses out of your personal funds. If you must pay any business expenses out of your own pocket or from your personal credit card, have the business reimburse you, so the business itself can claim the deductions.

Business reimbursements have their own set of IRS rules, requiring a written reimbursement policy, called an "accountable plan." This may require the help of an accountant.

Multiple Businesses

If you have more than one business, the IRS requires that you keep separate records and file separate tax forms for each business. You could, instead, choose to have only one business with several different "parts" or "divisions." With one business, you need to keep only one set of records and file one tax return.

If you do set up separate businesses or separate records for different parts of your business, shared expenses that apply to both businesses—such as office space, computer, telephone, employees working for both businesses—should be prorated between the businesses: 50–50 or any other split that reasonably approximates usage.

One Last Caution

Verify what you read in this book with a current IRS publication or with a competent accountant or attorney. Tax law is like quicksand, it's built on an ever-changing foundation. Congress is constantly screwing around with the tax laws. As soon as they pass another confusing law and promptly go on vacation, the IRS starts issuing interpretations of the law. And then some clever tax attorney finds a loophole, and the Tax Court gets to put in its two cents. Pretty soon, the law means something different than when first enacted.

The word, once printed, cannot be altered. Tax law, however, changes constantly. As a wise old carpenter once said, "Measure twice, cut once."

2

Terminology

There are many different terms for the same thing. Ten different businesses in ten different states may have ten different terms for a given business expense. To make this book as easy as possible to use, I have tried to list every term I know for every business deduction.

For example, you can look up "Goodwill" and find that it is also known as "Blue Sky." You can look up "Blue Sky" and find it is also known as "Goodwill." Employee benefits are explained under "Benefits" and "Fringe Benefits." This system results in some repetition and some duplication of definitions and explanations, but I think it makes the book faster and easier for people to use, and it eliminates the need to spend time poring through an index.

Here are a few important definitions you should know before getting any deeper into this book:

Self-Employed Individuals

Throughout this book, you will see the term "self-employed individuals." Self-employed individuals are in business for themselves. They are owners of sole proprietorships, partners in partnerships, and member/owners of limited liability companies (LLCs).

Independent contractors (also known as "outside contractors") are self-employed individuals. Freelancers, consultants, contractors, subcontractors, contract laborers, free agents, and other people in an independent trade or profession are self-employed individuals.

There is an important distinction between these self-employed individuals and people who have set up their businesses as corporations. People who own corporations, both regular C corporations and S corporations, are employees of their businesses. Although they are obviously self-employed, for tax purposes and for understanding the terminology in this book, they are not called self-employed individuals. They are referred to as employees, or if a distinction is important, as owner/employees.

In describing the tax deductions in this book, if the deductions are different for different types of businesses or different types of owners, the differences are explained. You will not have to guess if a deduction applies to you.

Employer/Employee

As you go through this book, be careful reading the last letter of these two words. The employer hires the employee. The employee works for the employer. The employer-employee relationship is a formal, legal relationship, with specific tax consequences. Tax deductions for employers are very different than for employees.

Independent contractors, contract laborers, and other self-employed individuals are not employees. If you hire these people, you are not their employer. If you are an independent contractor, the person or company hiring you is not your employer.

This book is careful to distinguish between employers, employees, and self-employed individuals (non-employees). You are cautioned to be equally careful.

What Is a Tax Deduction?

There are no dumb questions. A tax deduction is a dollar amount that is subtracted from your total business income (your total sales) in order to arrive at your taxable income, your net profit. The dollar amounts that you can deduct are known as "allowable business expenses."

An allowable business expense—a tax deduction—is not necessarily money you paid out this year. Some expenses are deductible the year paid. Some expenses are deducted over several years even though the cash was paid all in one year. Some expenses are only partially allowed. You may have a $100 expenditure but only a $50 tax deduction, because only half the expense is allowed by tax law. There are also business expenses—totally legitimate business expenses—that are not deductible at all. So, a tax deduction is what you can deduct, not necessarily what you spent.

This book explains which expenses are fully deductible the year paid, which expenses are deductible over several years, which expenses are only partly deductible, and which expenses are not deductible at all. I have tried to list and explain every possible business expense whether it is deductible or not.

Tax Write-Off

A tax write-off is another term for a tax deduction. The two terms are used interchangeably.

Personal vs. Business

A "personal" expense is a non-business expense, and it is not deductible on a business tax return. However, in tax law, the term "personal" has a second meaning. "Personal property" is any property other than real estate. "Personal property" includes machinery, equipment, furniture, and other assets a business owns. This "personal" property is actually business property, a business expense.

In the book, a "personal expense," refers to a non-business expense, not deductible on a business tax return. "Personal property" refers to business assets, not non-business assets. This is an important distinction, but you don't have to keep remembering it. Throughout the book, I try to point out the difference as it comes up.

Expenditures that are partly personal (non-business) and partly business can be prorated. The business portion is deductible.

Capitalized Expenses

In tax jargon, the term "capitalize" means that an asset or an expense cannot be deducted immediately. Such items are often called "capital assets" or "capital expenditures."

Some capital assets are deducted over a period of years, which is usually referred to as "depreciating" or "amortizing" the asset. Buildings and patents are two examples of assets that are "capitalized" and depreciated over many years.

Some capital assets cannot be deducted until sold. Land is an example of an asset that is "capitalized" and not deducted until sold.

Assets and expenses that must be capitalized are explained in the item list.

Audits

Throughout the book, I warn you about any deductions that might trigger IRS audits, and potential audit situations you should discuss with your accountant. So, what exactly is an IRS audit?

Every year, the IRS selects a small percentage of business tax returns to examine, looking to prove that the returns are accurate, that income is honestly stated, that deductions are legal. The IRS agents accomplish this task by talking to you or your accountant, by looking at your business records, and by examining your bank statements and business receipts.

Some audits are extensive; some are narrowly focused. Some audits will cover your entire business operation for the year, some audits may question only one or a few deductions.

At the conclusion of the audit, the IRS will report its findings to you and let you know if your tax bill increased, decreased, or remained unchanged.

Quite often, the IRS will find an error on a tax return when processing the return, typically an adding mistake or a tax calculation mistake. The IRS will automatically correct your return and notify you of your error and the increase or decrease in taxes. This kind of correction is not an audit. It does not increase or decrease your chances of being audited.

By the way, the term "audit" is no longer officially used by the IRS. According to the latest IRS press release, the IRS no longer "audits" tax returns. They, ah, "conduct examinations." The examinations, however, are identical to what the IRS used to call audits. Why the euphemism, I do not know. What I do know is, Fish is fish. An audit is an audit. And part of the goal of this book is to help you avoid an audit.

Tax Credits vs. Tax Deductions

Tax credits are listed in this book. Tax credits are different than tax deductions. A tax deduction reduces your net profit from your business. A tax credit does not reduce your net business profit, but it does reduce your income taxes. What is the difference?

You compute your business profit (your net profit) by taking your total income and subtracting from it your tax deductions, as explained above. You figure your tax based on this net profit.

After you compute your taxes, you then use any allowable tax credits to reduce those taxes. Again, a tax credit does not reduce your profit, it reduces the taxes on the profit.

For example, let's say you have a taxable profit of $40,000 for the year. If you are in, say, a 15 percent tax bracket, your income taxes are $6,000: 15 percent of $40,000. (I know that's simplifying tax calculations tremendously, but it makes the example a lot easier to explain.)

Then you read this book and find a $1,000 tax deduction you didn't know about. So you are able to write off an additional $1,000. Your profits are now $39,000 instead of $40,000 and your taxes are $5,850 instead of $6,000 (15 percent of $39,000 is $5,850). That $1,000 tax deduction saved you $150 in income taxes.

If, instead, the $1,000 you found by reading this book was a tax credit instead of a tax deduction, the computations are different. The tax credit does not reduce your profit. So you still have a $40,000 profit and a $6,000 tax bill. But then you reduce the $6,000 in taxes by the full $1,000 credit. Your taxes are now $5,000.

If you were able to follow this slightly confusing example, you'll see that a tax credit is more valuable than a tax deduction. In our example, the $1,000 tax deduction saved you $150 in taxes, but the $1,000 tax credit saved you a full $1,000 in taxes. The tax credit is a little gold mine, it is.

An item is either a tax deduction or a tax credit, not both.

Why does Congress offer both tax deductions and tax credits? To confuse the issues, of course. To make life more complicated for people trying to figure their taxes. To make accountants and tax lawyers rich. And because no one in Congress does his own tax return and has no idea how confusing the tax laws are. That's why.

That's not why. Most tax deductions are actual business expenses, the actual costs of running a business. Tax deductions tend to stay the same, year after year. Many tax credits have nothing to do with the actual expense of running a business. They are instead tax breaks to encourage you to do socially responsible things like hire people off welfare or to purchase equipment that will make for cleaner air and water. Some tax credits are meant to stimulate the economy. And some, believe it or not, just give you a much needed tax break, period.

So, send a letter of thanks to your congressperson for the self-employment tax credit, the health insurance tax credit, the tuition tax credit, the research and development tax credit, the oil drilling tax credit (that's right), and whatever else they've given us—or their corporate buddies—for Christmas this year.

Unlike tax deductions, tax credits tend to come and go, available one year and not the next. Congress has discovered that it is much easier to yank a tax credit they want to be rid of, than it is to drop a long-time tax deduction, which has been engraved on the stone tablets of tax law.

There is one more important difference between tax deductions and tax credits. Since tax deductions reduce your business profit, they also reduce your self-employment tax (Social Security and Medicare tax for self-employed individuals), which is approximately 15 percent of your profit. Tax credits, however, do not reduce your profit. So tax credits do not reduce your self-employment tax.

There are only a few tax credits and each one is specifically spelled out in tax law. By comparison, there are hundreds and hundreds of tax deductions, many of them not even mentioned in the IRS Tax Code, tax books, or tax forms at all.

In this book, tax credits are specifically labeled as such. If an item in this book does not say it is a tax credit, it is a tax deduction. If it doesn't say whether it is a tax deduction or a tax credit, it is a tax deduction. Read carefully.

3

The Four Basic Rules: All Expenses

Some business tax deductions are specifically spelled out in the IRS Tax Code: yes, you can deduct this, no you cannot deduct that. But the great majority of business deductions, most of the 475 tax deductions listed in this book, are not mentioned anywhere in the IRS code books. The law does not say, for example, that you can or cannot deduct pens for the office or light bulbs for the warehouse or bank service charges.

What the IRS does say, and says adamantly, is that all business expenses—and I mean *all expenses*, whether spelled out in the IRS code books or not—must meet four basic rules in order to be deductible:

1. The expenses must be incurred in connection with your trade, business, or profession.
2. The expenses must be "ordinary."
3. The expenses must be "necessary."
4. The expenses must "not be lavish or extravagant under the circumstances."

Any expense that does not meet all four of these requirements cannot be deducted on your business tax return.

The four basic rules, however, are not always as basic as they sound (of course). It is important for every business owner to understand a little more about these rules and, most important, to understand the definitions of the words as they are used in tax law. I am not going to confuse you here. These definitions, these tax laws, are not difficult to understand. If you will take five minutes to read these definitions, you will have a much greater understanding of tax law, and what you can legitimately deduct on your tax return.

Rule 1: Business Related

The expenses must be incurred in connection with your trade, business, or profession. The words "trade," "business," and "profession" are used interchangeably. All three refer to an activity carried on with a reasonable degree of regularity and with the sincere attempt to make a profit. It includes all self-employed individuals, sole proprietors, partners, members (owners) of Limited Liability Companies (LLCs), freelancers, independent contractors, free agents, and independent professionals. It includes full-time, part-time, and seasonal businesses. It includes Internet businesses.

"Reasonable degree of regularity" rules out occasional activities that bring in a little income. Such occasional activities are not considered a trade or business by the IRS.

"Sincere attempt to make a profit" rules out hobbies and other ventures done purely or mostly for the fun of it. There must be a real profit motive or the IRS says it is not a trade or business.

The expression "in connection with your trade or business" also means that you have already started a business. You must actually be in business before you are allowed to write off many business expenses. You are not allowed a deduction for business expenses incurred in connection with a business you are thinking of starting, planning to start some day, or researching in anticipation of starting.

You are allowed deductions for a business that you are actually starting, but have not yet opened your doors or made your first sale. The deductions, however, are limited and the rules are different. Before you incur any start-up costs, read the "Organizational Costs" and "Start-Up Costs" entries in chapter 4's A-to-Z section to find out how you can maximize your deductions.

Expenditures that are partly personal (non-business) and partly business can be prorated. The business portion is deductible. Any asset that you originally purchased and used for non-business purposes that you are now using for business or using partly for business is deductible.

Method of payment is immaterial. Payment can be made by cash, check, money order, credit card, debit card, or electronic transfer. If your business is a sole proprietorship, you can pay business expenses with a personal check, personal credit card, or debit card and get a business deduction. A business expense is deductible even if paid by a non-business check or credit card. But if you own a corporation or are in a partnership or limited liability company, the business should pay the bills. If you pay business expenses, the business should reimburse you.

Who the bill is made out to is also immaterial. If an invoice or a bill for a business expense is made out to you personally, instead of to your business, you still get a business deduction if the expense is a business expense.

If an expense is withheld from a payment to you (such as a self-employed real estate agent having split commissions deduction from income earned), the expense is deductible as though you had paid it yourself. You report the full amount of the money you earned, before the deduction, as taxable income, and you report the amount deducted as a business expense.

Special note to investors: Investing money—in other businesses, securities, commodities, the stock market—is not considered a trade or business by the IRS. Although people do invest with a "reasonable degree of regularity" and with the "sincere attempt to make a profit," investing does not meet the IRS definition of a trade or business. Sorry, you bought the wrong book. (This does not apply to people investing in their own businesses. You did buy the right book.)

Rule 2: Ordinary Expenses

The expenses must be "ordinary." An ordinary expense is one that is common or accepted in your type of business. Ordinary expenses do not have to be recurring or habitual.

Rule 3: Necessary Expenses

The expenses must be "necessary." A necessary expense, according to the IRS, is one "that is appropriate and helpful in developing and maintaining your trade or business."

It's important to understand that the word "necessary" in this context of IRS tax law does not have the same definition we usually associate with "necessary" as in "required," "indispensable," "must be done." It is not necessary that you buy nice stationery. It is not necessary that you air condition your office. These are not requirements for your business, but they pass the "necessary" test. An expense only has to be "appropriate and helpful" to meet the "necessary" test.

Rule 4: Not Lavish or Extravagant

The expenses must "not be lavish or extravagant under the circumstances."

Defining what is or is not "lavish or extravagant under the circumstances" depends on, well, depends on the circumstances. The bigger the business and the more income the business earns, the more likely you can deduct large amounts of money and call the expenses "not lavish or extravagant under the circumstances." Full-time, ongoing businesses can usually get away with a bit more lavishness than part-time and new businesses.

What if you are only working part time or just getting started? What if you have only a few clients? Would the IRS consider an expensive business trip extravagant? Most likely an IRS agent would be inclined to disallow such a deduction. But there is no clear answer to this question.

My own guideline: If you think a deduction might be considered lavish or extravagant, there is a good likelihood that it is. This is an area where I strongly advise you to get professional advice from a competent tax accountant.

There is no question that all four basic requirements are sometimes vague and subject to interpretation. The IRS, fortunately, tends to be quite reasonable about what's reasonable ("not lavish or extravagant"), as well as what is "ordinary" and "necessary." If the expense is business related, if it isn't outrageously extravagant, if it doesn't stick out on your tax return like a tuba in a string quartet, you are probably okay.

And remember, try to get receipts for everything, and keep them.

4

475 Tax Deductions for Home-Based Businesses, A–Z

From "Accountants" to "Zoning," these 475 listings are arranged in alphabetical order. Each deduction is defined and explained. Cross-references are in bold typeface. Special situations—such as rules specific to home businesses, manufacturers, corporations, employers, etc.—are labeled in bold and explained. The "Expense Category" suggests where to put the deduction on your tax form.

This alphabetical listing also includes tax credits, which are different than tax deductions (explained in chapter 2), and business expenses that are not deductible, just so you'll know.

Tax laws are complicated and unfriendly. Figuring out whether a home office can be deducted is a more difficult question than balancing the national budget. So most of us just give up and pay the full tax.

—Tom Person, Laughing Bear Newsletter, Houston, Texas

Accountants

It figures that the very first entry would be "accountants."

Accountants' fees are deductible. Business consultations with your accountant are deductible. Accounting, bookkeeping, payroll, tax return preparation, auditing, tax advice, and similar services are all deductible. Cost of hiring an accountant to help you with an IRS audit is deductible. Accounting software is deductible.

For preparing the tax return of a sole proprietor, only the cost of preparing the business part of the 1040 tax return (schedule C and related schedules) is deductible as a business expense. You should ask your accountant to separate out the fees for the business and personal parts of your tax return.

Expense category: Legal and professional services.

New businesses: Expenses incurred before starting your business come under special rules. See **Start-Up Costs**, **Organizational Costs**, **Buying a Business**.

Small businesses are very unhappy with the IRS. And I don't blame them.

—Charles O. Rossotti, Former IRS Commissioner

Accident Insurance

Accident insurance comes under the same rules as Health Insurance. See **Health Insurance**.

(Yes, I know, Accident should come before Accountant, but I did not want to start the book with "Accident.")

Advances

Advances paid to contractors, professionals, vendors, etc. are deductible. If the advance is a prepayment for work not yet done or goods not yet delivered, if it is a substantial amount of money, and if the advance applies to goods or services to be received next year, the deduction may have to be postponed to next year. See **Prepayments**.

If an advance is later refunded to you, and if you've already taken a deduction for it, you must reduce your current expenses or increase your gross income by the amount of the refund. Either way, the net effect is the same: to reverse the deduction you originally claimed.

Some advances are called deposits, but advances and deposits are not always the same thing. Generally, refundable deposits are not deductible. Non-refundable deposits are deductible. But like advances, deposits that are actually prepayments of some expense come under the prepaid expense rules. See **Prepayments**.

Expense category: Varies depending on actual expenses.

Advances to employees are considered regular taxable wages, subject to all payroll and withholding taxes.

Expense category: Wages.

Advertising

Advertising and promotional expenses are deductible. Advertising materials such as flyers and catalogs are deductible.

Expense category: Advertising.

Self-employed individuals often cheat themselves by considering an expense personal when it's really a business expense. In the corporate world, it's clear who is a business associate and who is not. For the self-employed, that line is very wiggly. Just because someone is a friend or family member doesn't mean he or she isn't a business associate.

—June Walker, financial writer

Air Conditioning

Air conditioning expenses for a home office are part of the Home Office deduction. Air conditioning costs for the entire home are prorated, business versus personal, using the same percentage as the home office. Air conditioning just for the office is fully deductible. If you take the flat rate ("safe harbor") Home Office deduction, air conditioning expenses are included in the flat rate. See **Home Office**.

Aircraft

Aircraft can be deducted the year of purchase, with limitations, or depreciated. See **Business Assets**, **Depreciation**. Leased aircraft can be deducted.

Expense category: Owned: Depreciation (also fill out Form 4562, "Depreciation and Amortization"). Leased: Rental expense.

Personal use: The cost of operating business aircraft used by business owners and employees for personal trips is deductible, though with limits, but the values of the flights are considered taxable wages. I suggest you talk to your accountant about this.

IRS Red Flag Audit Warning: Business deductions for aircraft will increase your likelihood of an audit. If audited, the IRS will request to see detailed records of the aircraft's use, looking for invalid deductions that were in fact personal, non-business expenses.

Air Fare

Deductible if certain requirements are met. See **Travel**.

Alarms

Alarm systems, both the purchase costs and any service fees, are part of the Home Office deduction. Alarm system costs for the entire home are prorated, business versus personal, using the same percentage as the home office. An alarm system just for the office is fully deductible. If you take the flat rate ("safe harbor") Home Office deduction, alarm systems expenses are included in the flat rate. See **Home Office**.

The problem is that my office is continually oozing out into the rest of the house. My financial department is currently in the dining room.

—Susan Jordan, owner, Magellan Medical Services

Allowance for Bad Debts

An allowance for bad debts, funds set aside in anticipation of a bad debt, is not deductible. Actual bad debts may or may not be deductible. See **Bad Debts**.

Amortization

Intangible assets such as trademarks and patents are deducted over a period of years. The deduction is called amortization. It is similar to depreciation; the procedure is the same. See **Depreciation**.

Expense category: Depreciation (also fill out Form 4562, "Depreciation and Amortization").

Trademark: If you acquire rights to a trademark from another business, under a licensing agreement, the payments are deductible when paid. They do not have to be amortized.

Expense category: Other expenses.

Loan amortization: The term amortization also refers to paying off a loan. Loan amortization is not a deductible expense. A loan is not income when you get it and is not an expense when you pay it off. Any interest is deductible. See **Interest Expense**.

Answering Service

Telephone answering service fees are deductible. Any initial setup or installation charges are also deductible.

Expense category: Office expense, or Legal and professional services.

Just remember, the business belongs to you, not your accountant.

—Gloria Gibbs Marullo, business columnist and CPA

Antiques

Valuable antiques, if used for decoration only, may not be depreciated and cannot be deducted until sold.

The Tax Court, however, has ruled that antiques actually used in the business, such as an old desk, or a professional musician's rare violin, can be depreciated or, at your option, deducted the year of purchase (up to a maximum amount), but only if the items can wear out or deteriorate from use. (See **Business Assets, Depreciation.**) The IRS disagrees, and has stated that no rare and valuable antiques can be written off until sold, regardless of how they are used. If you have significant money at stake, I suggest you talk to your accountant.

Expense category: Depreciation (if deductible). Also fill out Form 4562, "Depreciation and Amortization."

Dealers in antiques treat antiques as inventory. See **Inventory**.

Appraisal Fees

Appraisal fees paid to determine the amount of a loss are deductible. Appraisal fees paid to determine a value on a donated item are deductible (for corporations only—see **Donations**). Appraisal fees involving the purchase or sale of a business may have to be capitalized (deducted over several years). See **Start-Up Costs**.

Expense category: Legal and professional services.

Apps

Apps (application software) for smartphones are 100 percent deductible if used 100 percent for business. If used partly for business, you can deduct the percentage of the cost used for business.

Expense category: Office expenses.

If more people knew what a small percentage of tax returns we actually audit, we'd have an enormous number of taxpayers playing audit roulette.

—Jerome Kurtz, Former IRS Commissioner

Architectural Firms

Some architectural firms are eligible for the Domestic Production Deduction, also known as the Manufacturer's Deduction. See **Manufacturer's Deduction**.

Art Treasures

Art treasures are not deductible. The IRS states that these objects do not depreciate in value, so no deduction or depreciation is allowed. You report a profit or loss on the items when you sell them.

Dealers in art treasures treat art treasures as inventory. See **Inventory.**

Assessments

Local government assessments for streets, sidewalks, water lines, sewers, and the like are part of the Home Office deduction. Assessments that apply to the entire home are prorated, business versus personal, using the same percentage as the home office. If you take the flat rate ("safe harbor") Home Office deduction, home-related assessments are included in the flat rate. See **Home Office.**

Assessments unrelated to the home office are deductible, depending on what they are for. Look up individual items.

Assets

Business assets can be deducted the year of purchase, with limitations, or depreciated over a period of years. See **Business Assets.**

Once a month I venture into rush hour traffic to remind myself of what I'm missing.

—Jeannette Scollard, SCS Manufacturing

Associations

Dues and other expenses for business groups, professional organizations, merchant and trade associations, business leagues, unions, chambers of commerce, etc. are deductible. Dues to community service organizations, such as Rotary, Lions, Kiwanis, etc., are deductible.

Expense category: Other expenses.

Dues and membership fees in clubs run for pleasure, recreation, or other social purposes are not deductible. These include athletic, luncheon, hotel, airline, sporting, and other entertainment or recreational organizations, associations, clubs, and facilities. Even if you use a club membership solely to generate or discuss business, the dues are not deductible. Sometimes the term "business club" is used to describe such a facility. If the "business" club is not a business organization, the dues are not deductible.

ATM Fees

ATM (automatic teller machine) fees are deductible.

Expense category: Office expenses.

Blaming the IRS is a lot like blaming the doctor whose patient has an incurable disease. Tax reform, not IRS bashing, is the only way to liberate the American people from a system that is grotesquely burdensome and monstrous.

—Fred Goldberg, Former IRS Commissioner

Attorneys

Attorney's fees are deductible, but see exceptions below.

Expense category: Legal and professional services.

Exceptions: Expenses incurred before starting your business and expenses associated with buying a business come under special rules. See **Start-Up Costs**, **Organizational Costs**, **Buying a Business**. Attorney fees related to business mergers or acquisitions must be capitalized.

Audits

The cost of an audit by an accounting firm or auditing service is deductible. The cost of hiring an accountant or lawyer to defend yourself in an IRS audit of your business is deductible. Any taxes or penalties are not deductible. Interest on back taxes is not deductible except for corporations.

Expense category: Legal and professional services.

Automobiles

Cars used for business can be deducted or depreciated, but with certain limitations. See **Vehicles**.

Expense category: The category "Car and truck expenses" is for all vehicle expenses except the cost of the vehicle itself, which is deducted or depreciated under "Depreciation." See **Depreciation**.

Leased automobiles: Automobile leases, if 30 days or longer, are not 100 percent deductible. The IRS has a table called "Inclusion Amounts for Cars" that shows how much of an auto lease can be deducted. See IRS Publication 463 for the table. This rule does not apply to trucks, vans, or heavy sport utility vehicles.

If you can run a home-based business and have nobody realize it unless you tell them, then you're doing it right.

—Sean Spoonts, Patriot Group Inc., Puntagorda, Florida

Awards

Awards to employees: Awards (and prizes and bonuses) paid to employees are considered wages subject to all payroll taxes. Awards are deductible like all employee wages. Awards can be in cash, gift certificates, or goods; the same rules apply. However, small token awards of merchandise—not cash—to employees are not taxable to the employee.

There is one exception to the awards rule. The IRS recognizes something they call an "employee achievement award." Up to $400 per year can be given to an employee, tax free, as an employee achievement award, and the employer gets a deduction. The maximum increases to $1,600 a year if you have an IRS-approved "qualified plan." You will probably need help from your accountant to set up such a plan.

Employee achievement awards are for length of service or for safety, but not for things like top salesperson of the month or extra hours worked. Employee achievement awards cannot be "disguised compensation."

Expense category: Wages.

Awards to non-employees: Incentive awards and prizes to customers or suppliers are deductible within limits, but the law can be very confusing on this. There is a fine line between a business "gift" (with a $25 limit; see **Business Gifts**) and a business "award" or "prize" (not limited to $25). The IRS usually considers a "thank you" after the transaction is completed to be a gift, but considers an incentive to do business to be an award. There is also a problem that the award may possibly be taxable to the recipient. This is a common situation for real estate agents who often give home buyers a new washer or refrigerator as part of the sales deal. I suggest you talk to your accountant before you give a gift or an award, so you structure the transaction—and the terminology—to your best tax advantage.

Expense category: Advertising, or Other expenses.

Lots of things can happen if you don't keep the right records, and none of them are good.

—Dan Smogor, CPA

Babysitting

Self-employed individuals cannot deduct the cost of babysitting or caring for their own children, unless you are an employee of your own corporation. Employers can deduct dependent care expenses for their employees. See **Dependent Care**.

Bad Checks

Deductible. See **Bounced Checks**.
Expense category: Bad debts.

Bad Debts

Some bad debts are deductible. These include customers' bounced checks and credit card charges customers refuse to pay.

If you sell on account to customers, any uncollectible accounts are deductible, but only if they were posted to your income ledger when you made the sale. Businesses using the cash method of accounting (recording income when the money comes in, not when the sale was made) cannot take a bad debt expense for uncollectible accounts, because the income was not recorded in the first place. You get a bad debt deduction only if you recorded income in your income ledger that you are unable to collect.

A self-employed individual cannot take a bad debt deduction for his or her own time devoted to a client or customer who doesn't pay. You do not get a deduction for the income you should have earned, the money you were cheated out of. I know that doesn't sound fair, and it isn't, but that is how the tax laws are written. You are out the money you should have earned, and the IRS says, Tough Luck.

You do get a deduction for any inventory (goods) you sold that you didn't get paid for. Inventory is deducted at the end of the year as part of cost-of-goods-sold. See **Inventory**.

Deduct only those bad debts that you are certain are uncollectible. The bad debts should be specifically identified. Amounts cannot be estimated. If you are unsure, you can wait until next year. You can write off a bad debt in any future year that it becomes definitely uncollectible.

Expense category: Bad debts.

Bad Debt Reserves: A few businesses that anticipate large bad debts sometimes set aside money in a bad debt reserve fund, sort of like self-insurance. Such reserves are not really business expenses and are not tax deductible.

Remember, the goal is to work at home, not to feel like you live at work.

—Jacqueline Lynn, business writer

Bail Bond Fees

Business-related bail bond fees may be deductible, if they meet the IRS's "ordinary" and "necessary" tests. You should ask your accountant about this. Bail bond fees are not legal fines or legal penalties, which are not deductible.

Expense category: Legal and professional services.

Bank Charges

Bank charges, services, ATM fees, penalties, check writing and credit card fees, are deductible. Check printing costs are deductible.

Expense category: Office expenses.

Bankruptcy

Cost of filing for bankruptcy and related expenses are deductible.

Expense category: Legal and professional services.

Customer bankruptcy: If one of your customers files for bankruptcy, and you are unable to collect money owed to you, you will have a bad debt expense, deductible unless you are on the cash basis of accounting. See **Bad Debts**. Any expenses you incur to try to collect the debts are deductible. If a supplier goes bankrupt, and if you have paid for goods or services not delivered, you can deduct your loss as a bad debt.

Expense category: Bad debts.

Government isn't religion. It shouldn't be treated as such. It's humans, fallible people, feathering their nests most of the time.

—Jerry Brown, Governor of California

Barter

"In the beginning, there was no money." But there always was the tax man, and barter does not escape his grasp. Barter transactions are taxable just like all other business transactions.

When you exchange or trade your business goods or services for someone else's goods or services, it is called barter. The "fair market value" of the goods or services you receive must be included in your regular business income and treated just like any other business income.

"Fair market value" is what you would have normally paid for the goods or services in the normal course of business ("arm's length transaction"), had you been paying cash.

If the goods or services you receive are used in your business, you get a business deduction on your taxes, just as though you paid cash. You deduct the fair market value of the goods or services received.

If you join a barter club (exchange, network), the rules are basically the same. Barter club commissions and fees are deductible. Barter clubs report all transactions to the IRS. In IRS audits of businesses, one of the first questions often asked is, "Do you engage in trade or barter?" A yes answer is a red flag to expand the scope of the audit to include items of unreported income.

Businesses that deal in "virtual currency" such as Bitcoins are conducting business identical to barter transactions as far as the IRS and tax law is concerned. See **Bitcoins**.

Expense category: Depends on what is acquired in trade.

My home is corporate headquarters. The nerve center of our company is the laundry room. It houses the company's file server, fax machine, alarm system, credit card processing equipment, washer, and dryer. At night, with all the lights flashing, it looks like the deck of the Starship Enterprise.

—Glen Paul, cofounder, QwikQuote Development

Benefits

Employers can deduct the cost of employee fringe benefits, with some exceptions and limits. Fringe benefits for you, the owner of the business, and for your family may or may not be deductible depending on how your business is structured.

See **Awards, Business Gifts, Dependent Care, Discounts, Education Expenses, Health Insurance, Life Insurance, Medical Expenses, Parking, Retirement Plans**.

Expense category: Employee benefit programs.

Billboards

Rental costs for billboards are deductible. Billboards you own can be deducted (up to a maximum amount) or depreciated. See **Business Assets, Depreciation**.

Expense category: Rent or lease; or Depreciation (also fill out Form 4562, "Depreciation and Amortization").

Bitcoins

Business expenses paid in Bitcoins and other virtual currencies are deductible exactly the same as expenses paid in U.S. currency. The amount of the expense is the fair market value of the Bitcoins at the time of the transaction. This is identical to the IRS rules regarding Barter. See **Barter**.

Expense category depends on the type of expense.

Blue Sky

Another term for goodwill, an intangible asset. If purchased as part of the purchase price of a business, it must be amortized (depreciated) over a period of years. See **Goodwill**.

Expense category: Depreciation (also fill out Form 4562, "Depreciation and Amortization").

Just be glad you aren't getting all the government you're paying for.

—Will Rogers, cowboy philosopher

Boats

Boats, if needed for your business, can be deducted the year of purchase, with limitations, or depreciated. See **Business Assets, Depreciation**. Boats used for recreation or entertainment are usually not deductible even if they are used only for business purposes.

Boats, as you can imagine, are likely to raise IRS eyebrows. If you deduct your boat, your odds of being audited are increased significantly.

Expense category: Depreciation (also fill out Form 4562, "Depreciation and Amortization").

Boat as a home office: If you live on a boat and use part of it for a home office, the boat is part of the Home Office deduction. Rent or depreciation on the boat is prorated, business versus personal, using the same percentage as the home office. If you take the flat rate ("safe harbor") Home Office deduction, boat expenses are included in the flat rate. See **Home Office**.

Bodyguard

(1) If needing a bodyguard is an ordinary and necessary expense of your business, it is a deductible expense. (2) If needing a bodyguard is an ordinary and necessary expense of your business, I would suggest you start a different business.

Expense category: Other expenses.

Bonds

Surety Bonds: There is a type of insurance called a surety bond. If you do not complete a job, for any reason, your surety company must do so. Many service businesses such as auto repair shops and many building contractors are required by law to have surety bonds. The cost of surety bonds is deductible.

Fidelity Bonds: There is a type of insurance called a fidelity bond. Fidelity bonds are placed on employees, insuring against theft or embezzlement by the bonded employees. If you have employees going into people's homes and businesses, such as a janitorial service, a fidelity bond protects you and the client should one of your employees turn out to be a thief. The cost of fidelity bonds is deductible.

Expense category: Insurance.

Interest Bearing Bonds: There are monetary documents called bonds, interest bearing instruments (as they are often called) similar to notes or loans. The bonds themselves are not deductible. The interest is deductible.

Expense category: Interest.

Also see **Bail Bond Fees**.

It's hard to work when your kids are at home. You want to be with them. They want you. Or they want pizza. What are you going to do? You can't stick them in front of a video for more than 22 consecutive hours.

—Peggy Edersheim, Work and Family

Bonus (Employers)

Bonuses paid to employees are considered wages subject to all payroll taxes and laws. Bonuses are deductible, just like all employee wages. Also see **Awards**.

Expense category: Wages.

A cash gift to an employee (or cash equivalent, such as a gift certificate) is treated like a bonus, taxable wages. Small, non-cash gifts to employees are not taxable to the employees, and are deductible by the employer. See **Business Gifts**.

Bookkeeping

Bookkeeping services and software are deductible. See **Record Keeping**.

Books

Books, magazines, newsletters, newspapers, and all other publications are deductible. The cost of buying and maintaining your books (ledgers) is deductible.

Expense category: Office expenses (for publications). Legal and professional services (for bookkeeping).

From a tax lawyer's point of view, we're in heaven.

—Leslie B. Samuels, tax attorney

Bounced Checks

Bounced checks are deductible; that is, the ones your lousy customers bounce on you.

Expense category: Bad debts.

Your own bounced checks, the ones you wrote, are not deductible. Because nothing was actually paid, right? That makes sense, doesn't it? Bank charges and penalties are deductible. Any legal fines are not deductible.

Expense category: Office expense.

Boxes

Boxes, cartons, and other containers and packaging materials that hold the goods you sell, are considered part of your inventory and are included in cost of goods sold. See **Inventory**. If, however, the cost of the boxes is not significant or if used only occasionally, most businesses deduct the costs currently as shipping supplies.

Expense category: Supplies.

My business is run out of my home. For display, I completely remodeled my kitchen with every kind of cabinet, an island with a cook top, an archway into the dining area, and a deck behind the kitchen. It has helped sell quite a few kitchens, plus we enjoy the luxury.

—Michael Karna, Karna Construction Company

Bribes

It is illegal to bribe a U.S. or foreign government official. It is illegal to offer a bribe to win a foreign contract. Illegal payments are not deductible.

But some bribes are legal, and legal bribes are deductible. The federal government has no laws against bribing a company official, a purchasing agent, a sales rep, etc. But your state may outlaw these bribes. If the bribe is illegal in your state, no deduction. The IRS goes by state laws on this deduction.

By the way, business gifts are deductible, up to $25 per recipient per year. See **Business Gifts**. Is a gift a bribe? Is a bribe a gift?

Expense category: If legal, Other expenses.

Broker's Fees

A broker's fee to buy or sell real estate usually must be added to the value of the real estate. See **Buildings**. A broker's fee as part of buying or selling a business usually must be added to the cost of the business. See **Buying A Business**.

Any other broker's fee paid in the normal course of business (other than the two situations above) is deductible.

Expense category: Legal and professional services.

It's not a loophole, it's the law.

—Joseph Lents, accountant

Building Components

Building components are part of the **Home Office** deduction. Building components that are part of the entire home are prorated, business versus personal, using the same percentage as the home office. Building components that are for the business only—such as awnings, partitions, air conditioning—are fully deductible. Most building components must be depreciated over the life of the building, but there are exceptions. If you take the flat rate ("safe harbor") Home Office deduction, building components are included in the flat rate.

See **Home Office**.

Buildings

The building that houses your home office is part of the **Home Office** deduction. You can deduct the business portion of the rent if you rent your home, or the business portion of the depreciation if you own your home. Homeowners who depreciate the business part of their homes should be especially aware of tax problems that can come up when you sell the home. This is a very important issue, covered under **Home Office**. If you take the flat rate ("safe harbor") Home Office deduction, building rent or depreciation is included in the flat rate. See **Home Office**. Also see **Interest Expense, Property Taxes.**

Other buildings that you use for business, such as a warehouse, salesroom, or workshop located away from your home, can be depreciated in addition to taking the Home Office deduction. See **Depreciation**. However, you want to be careful how you define the buildings' uses so that you don't lose the Home Office deduction.

Land: The land under the building cannot be depreciated or deducted. You get no tax deduction until you sell the land.

Rehabilitation Tax Credit: If you are rehabilitating a certified historic building or a building built before 1936, for use in your business, you may be eligible for a special tax credit, in addition to the regular depreciation deduction. See **Tax Credits**.

Disabled Access Credit: If you renovate your workplace to accommodate people with disabilities, you may be eligible for a special tax credit, in addition to the regular depreciation deduction. See **Tax Credits**.

Energy efficiency improvements: Some expenses that reduce the energy usage in commercial buildings can be written off instead of depreciated. The rules are very specific, and will require help from a tax accountant.

Real estate developers: Pre-development costs such as planning and design, blueprints, building permits, engineering studies, landscape plans, and the like, cannot be deducted currently, but must be capitalized. If you construct low-income housing, you may be eligible for a Low Income Housing Tax Credit. See **Tax Credits**.

It's hard to conduct a business in your spare time. Nobody has spare time.

—Peggy Morris, home-based business owner, Savoy International, Inc.

Business Assets

Tangible business assets such as machinery, equipment, tools, furniture, fixtures, leasehold improvements, display cases, office machines, vehicles, and software, can (with some exceptions) be deducted the year of purchase. This is often referred to as the "First-Year Write-Off" or the "Section 179 Deduction" (referring to a section in the Internal Revenue Code). The maximum deduction under this rule, all assets combined, is $25,000. This maximum changes from year to year.

The First-Year Write-Off of business assets is optional. If you prefer, you can depreciate some or all of these assets over a period of years rather than deducting them the year of purchase. If you owe little or no income tax this year, it might be worth depreciating the assets, spreading the deduction over several years to get a better tax savings in the future. See **Depreciation**.

There are many details and restrictions to this first-year-write-off rule:

1. Both new and used assets qualify as long as they were purchased for the business and not before going into business. Assets used in your business that were purchased before going into business must be depreciated.
2. This write-off rule does not apply to intangible assets such as patents, copyrights, trademarks, goodwill, etc.

3. This rule does not apply to buildings, although there are a few exceptions.

4. This rule does not apply to inventory, parts, manufacturing supplies, office supplies, or other consumables.

5. Some vehicles, even if used 100 percent for business, have a much lower maximum deduction than other assets. See "Limitations on Vehicles" under **Depreciation**.

6. For married couples, the deduction for both spouses combined cannot exceed the maximum.

7. If you have more than one unincorporated business, the deduction for all of your unincorporated businesses combined cannot exceed the maximum.

8. The annual maximum is reduced if the cost of the assets you purchase, all assets combined, exceed $200,000. This maximum changes from year to year.

9. The deduction cannot exceed the total taxable income from all unincorporated businesses and salaries combined (both husband and wife if filing jointly). Any deduction disallowed because of this limitation can be carried forward to the next year, and future years if necessary, until the assets are fully written off.

10. If an asset is used partly for business and partly for non-business use, business use must be over 50 percent to be eligible for this deduction. Assets used 50 percent or less for business must be depreciated (business portion only).

11. Assets do not have to be paid for to qualify. Assets qualify if they are placed in service during the year.

12. If you sell assets you've previously deducted, or convert them to non-business use, you may have to "recapture" the amount you deducted (add it back into income) the year of sale or conversion, depending on how many years you own the asset.

Assets ineligible for this First-Year Write-Off, or in excess of the maximums, can be depreciated. See **Depreciation**. For more information on Business Assets, see IRS Publication 946, "How to Depreciate Property."

Expense category: Depreciation (also fill out Form 4562, "Depreciation and Amortization").

Licensing businesses: Photographers, illustrators, software developers, and others who license their work can usually write off their expenses.

Disabled Access Credit: Some equipment, if purchased to assist disabled employees or customers (such as a physical therapist's hydraulic table) is eligible for the Disabled Access Tax Credit. See **Tax Credits**.

In America, there are two tax systems: one for the informed, and one for the uninformed. Both are legal.

—Judge Learned Hand

Business Associations

Dues and meetings are deductible. See **Dues, Travel, Meals, Lodging**.

Expense category: Other expenses.

Business Cards

Business cards are deductible.

Expense category: Office expense.

Business Gifts

Tax deductions for business gifts are limited to $25 per recipient in any one year. Gifts to business entities such as a gift to a corporation, if not given to specific individuals, are fully deductible; no $25 maximum.

Samples of your merchandise, given to prospective buyers or to people who might review or publicize your products, are not considered gifts and are not subject to these gift limitations. You write off the cost of the free samples (not the retail or market value) as part of cost-of-goods sold. See **Inventory**.

Expense category: Other expenses.

Gifts to employees: Money, "cash equivalents" such as gift certificates, and items of significant value, are considered taxable wages, subject to payroll taxes. Small non-monetary gifts, such as a Thanksgiving turkey or a birthday gift, are deductible and are not considered part of the employee's wages. Gifts to employees are not subject to the $25 cost limit.

Awards: Incentive awards and prizes to customers are not business "gifts" and are not subject to the $25 limitation. But the law can be very confusing on this. See **Awards**.

When I first started working from home, I tried to block off time when I would work and do nothing else. But I quickly realized that didn't cut it for me. Ideas flow whether I'm in or out of my work area. I need to be able to work on my home to-do list when I'm in my office, and I need to answer a business call when I'm outside playing with my dog.

—Diana Salerno, marketing consultant, Houston, Texas

Business Licenses

Business licenses, registrations, and similar fees are deductible.
Expense category: Taxes and licenses.

Business Opportunity

See **Buying a Business**.

Business Trips

Business trips are usually deductible, but there are many rules and restrictions. See **Travel**.
Expense category: Travel.

Busses

Busses and large transporters used for business can be deducted or depreciated like other vehicles. Vehicles have special limitations. See **Vehicles**.

Expense category: The category "Car and truck expenses" is for all vehicle expenses except the cost of the vehicle itself, which is deducted or depreciated under "Depreciation."

Bus as home office: If you are living in a bus, the office space can be deducted if it meets the home office requirements. If the bus is parked on your home property, being used for business, it is also eligible for the home office deduction. See **Home Office**.

Buying a Business

There are four ways someone might buy a business: 1. Purchasing a business from the former owner of the business. 2. Buying a franchise, where you become a franchisee, purchasing the right to the franchise name and operating as though your business was part of a much larger operation. 3. Buying into a direct-sales (multi-level, networking) program, usually where you buy and resell consumer goods, often cosmetics or vitamins or kitchen wares. 4. Buying a "business opportunity," where you purchase a start-your-own-business "kit" that includes training guides, and possibly inventory and equipment.

Buying an Independent Business

When you buy someone else's business, some of the purchase price is deductible, some of the cost is depreciated or amortized over several years, some of the cost may not be deductible at all. A lot depends on how the business is structured legally (corporation, partnership, limited liability company, or sole proprietorship) and what the purchase agreement says. The precise legal wording can affect how the sale is taxed, how the assets are valued for tax purposes, and how much of the purchase price will be deductible.

For most business purchases, you are not actually buying a "business," you are buying a collection of assets that comprise a business: equipment, furniture and fixtures, inventory, supplies, possibly a building, possibly the accounts receivable, possibly the debts and liabilities. The purchase price sometimes includes a "covenant not to compete": the seller agrees not to start another business that will be in competition with the one you are buying.

You may also be buying what's called goodwill, money you are paying above the actual value of the assets. An ongoing, successful business is worth more than a new, untested business. That "worth more" is the goodwill, obviously a very subjective value.

Each component of the business (assets, inventory, goodwill, etc.) is valued separately, and each component comes under different tax deduction rules. A lot of tax money is at stake here. You should talk to an experienced tax accountant before signing any agreement.

Expense category: Depends on what is being purchased.

Buying a Franchise, Business Opportunity, or Direct Sales Distributorship

Tax deductions for buying a franchise or other prepackaged business opportunity depend on what you are actually purchasing. A one-time fee to become a franchisee or distributor is considered an intangible asset, and is amortized over 15 years. See **Depreciation**. Ongoing (annual) franchise or distributor fees can be written off when paid (Expense category: Commissions and Fees). Costs for equipment, inventory, and supplies are deducted under the rules for the specific items you are purchasing.

A business broker's commission for helping to buy or sell a business may have to be amortized (depreciated) over five years. See **Depreciation**.

Also see **Start-Up Costs, Organizational Costs**.

---

77 percent of small businesses polled think the existing tax system should be scrapped.

—National Small Business United

Cafeteria Plan (Employers)

This is a term for an employee fringe benefit plan, also known as a Flexible Spending Account, where you can reimburse employees' medical and child care expenses. Employees gets to choose from several fringe-benefit options, sort of like choosing food from a cafeteria.

If set up properly, the costs of a cafeteria plan are deductible to you, the employer, and not taxable to your employees. This will require the help of an experienced accountant.

Expense category: Employee benefit programs.

Campaign Contributions

Not deductible. See **Political Contributions**.

The good news about working from home is that you can be close to your loved ones. That's also the bad news.

—Amy Dunkin, home-business owner

Cancellation Penalties

Deductible.
Expense category: Other expenses.

Capital Assets

Capital assets are more commonly known as business assets, fixed assets, or depreciable assets. They include machinery, equipment, furniture, etc: assets that are used in the business.

Some capital assets can be deducted the year purchased, some must be depreciated over several years. See **Business Assets**, **Depreciation**.

Expense category: Depreciation (also fill out Form 4562, "Depreciation and Amortization").

Carrying Charges

A carrying charge is a service charge or financing charge for buying something on time, or in installments, or on layaway. Carrying charges are treated like interest charges and are usually deductible. See **Interest**.

Expense category: Interest.

Pay my "fair share" of taxes? That sounds like something coming out of Moscow, you know, their "fair share." Karl Marx talked like that. Is there going to be Big Brother that's going to decide what your "fair share" is? That is not a concept that's contained in the Internal Revenue Code.

—Bill Simon, multimillionaire and former candidate for governor of California, when asked if he paid any California taxes

---

Cartons

Cartons, boxes, and other containers and packaging that are used to hold the goods you sell, are considered part of your inventory and included in cost-of-goods-sold. See **Inventory**.

If, however, the cost of the containers or packaging is not significant or they are used only occasionally, most businesses write them off currently as shipping supplies or office supplies.

Expense category: Supplies.

Casualty Losses

Business losses from fire, storm or other casualty, or from theft, shoplifting, or vandalism are deductible to the extent they are not covered by insurance. However, there are different rules for different types of losses and different types of businesses.

For businesses other than C corporations, most thefts and casualties are deductible on the business owner's 1040 tax return, not on the business return. The only exception to this rule is theft of inventory. Inventory loss is deducted as part of your cost-of-goods-sold. See **Inventory**.

Stolen or destroyed depreciable property (business assets that you are depreciating) can be deducted as a casualty loss, but only to the extent of the undepreciated balance. The portion you already depreciated was deducted as a depreciation expense in prior years, and cannot be deducted a second time. If you wrote the entire asset off the first year, you have no deductible loss.

For more information, see IRS Publication 547, "Casualties, Disasters and Thefts." Also see the instructions for Form 4684, "Casualties and Thefts."

Expense category: Depends on what kind of property is affected.

Cell Phones

Cell (cellular) phones, smartphones, and mobile phones, if used 100 percent for business, are 100 percent deductible. This includes the cost of the phone, cost of any contract, and the usage fees. But you must keep detailed records on the cell phone usage (time, place, business purpose of calls) to get the deduction. Many cell companies offer detailed call-by-call bills to assist you with the record keeping.

If your cell phone is used partly for business, you can deduct the percentage of the cost used for business.

Expense category: Office expenses.

Service contract: If you have a service contract, it can be added to the cost of the phone, or it can be deducted separately, as a repair expense. See **Repairs**.

It's possible to resist the widespread impulse to furnish your home office with the latest, fastest technology if, one, you know your work doesn't require it, and two, you have no intention of ever inviting clients over to see how low-rent your equipment is.

—Doug Stewart, home-business owner

Charitable Contributions

Only corporations can deduct charitable contributions and donations as a business deduction, and only if the charities have IRS charitable non-profit status. Corporations can deduct up to 10 percent of their taxable income. Contributions must be substantiated by a cancelled check, bank record, or receipt from the recipient.

Corporations that donate used equipment, furniture, or other depreciable assets cannot claim a deduction if the assets are already depreciated or written off.

C corporations (not S corporations) that donate inventory to qualified charities can get a deduction for more than the cost of the inventory. They can deduct the cost plus half the difference between cost and regular sales price, up to twice the cost of the inventory.

Expense category: Charitable contributions (corporations only).

Businesses other than corporations: Sole proprietorships, partnerships, and limited liability companies may not take deductions for charitable contributions. The owners of these businesses may be able to deduct charitable contributions on their personal 1040 returns.

However, instead of making a non-deductible donation to a charity, if your business purchases an advertisement in a charitable organization's directory or event program, the cost of the ad (if "reasonable") is fully deductible. If your business sponsors a charitable organization's team or event, the sponsorship is deductible.

Expense category: Advertising.

Charitable contribution as promotion: In a recent IRS ruling, a business donated money to a charitable organization, and as a result got favorable publicity. The donation was not deductible as a charitable contribution, because it did not meet IRS requirements. But the donation was fully deductible as an advertising cost. This may be a way around deduction limitations on some charitable contributions. You should ask your accountant about this possible tax deduction.

Expense category: Advertising.

People will do silly things to avoid taxes.

—J. C. Small, tax attorney, counsel to the director, New Jersey Division of Taxation

---

Chauffeur

As I discussed in the beginning of this book, all business expenses, in order to be deductible, must meet three IRS requirements. They must be (1) ordinary, (2) necessary, and (3) not lavish or extravagant. If you can look an underpaid, underappreciated IRS agent in the eye, and convince him that the cost of hiring your personal chauffeur is ordinary, necessary, and not lavish or extravagant, I congratulate you.

Seriously though, there may well be a business situation where you want to make an impression on a client, where a chauffeur is appropriate, and deductible. Beware that you may be walking a fine line between promoting your business, which is fully deductible, and "entertainment," which is only 50 percent deductible. You may want to discuss this deduction with your tax accountant. Actually, I'd suggest that you just not take the deduction, period.

Expense category: Legal and professional services.

The home-based business is the last refuge from the bureaucratic meddling and stifling protectionism that inevitably accompany any and all government involvement. Those who long for government action on their behalf would do well to remember the axiom, "For every government action, there is an overwhelming and destructive reaction."

—Norman D. Wood, home-business owner

Child Care

Self-employed individuals cannot deduct the cost of child care for their own children, unless you are an employee of your own corporation. Employers can deduct child care expenses for their employees. See **Dependent Care**.

Child care business: Expenses for running a child care business are deductible like the expenses of any other business. If you run a child care business out of your home, see **Home Office** for special child care deductions allowed.

Children on Payroll

You can hire your children, get a deduction for their wages, and— within certain limitations—the children are not subject to income or payroll taxes.

The rules are very specific, but generally, if your child is under eighteen and does legitimate work for your business, you can pay each of your children who qualify up to $6,200 a year tax free and get a business deduction for the wages. The maximum amount changes from year to year; it is the same as the standard deduction for unmarried individuals.

The children do not have to file a federal income tax return, and owe no federal income taxes. And you, the parent-employer get a full tax deduction for the wages paid. It's a rare tax law indeed that lets you have your cake and eat it too.

This deduction for your children applies only to sole proprietorships, spousal partnerships, and one-person LLCs filing as sole proprietors, and it has a lot of variables. If your child has what's called "unearned income," such as bank interest, it cannot exceed $1,000; and the child's total income, wages and all other taxable sources, cannot exceed $6,200.

If the child does have excess unearned income, or if the child is earning more than the $6,200 income maximum, the child must file an income tax return. But the child's wages, regardless of the amount paid, are exempt from federal payroll taxes (Social Security /Medicare taxes).

For more information, see IRS Publication #15, "Circular E, Employer's Tax Guide."

Check with your state employment department before you hire your children. Many states have laws similar to the IRS, impose no state income or payroll taxes, nor require worker's compensation insurance on your children. Check your state employer's guide. Do not rely on verbal information. People who work at state employment departments are often unaware of child employment laws.

Your children must have a W-4 payroll form on file (does not need to be sent to the IRS), and you must file W-2 and W-3 payroll forms, as you would for any employee, but no payroll taxes are due. You do not need to file a 941 or 944 payroll tax return.

Expense category: Wages.

Children who hire their parents: The parents are considered regular employees, subject to all regular employment and income taxes, except Federal Unemployment Tax (FUTA). Parents are exempt from FUTA.

Brilliant deduction, Dr. Watson.

—Sherlock Holmes

Classes

Many classes and education expenses are deductible. See **Education Expenses**.
Expense category: Other expenses.

Cleaning Service

Office: Cleaning and janitorial services are part of the **Home Office** deduction. Cleaning services for the entire home are prorated, business versus personal, using the same percentage as the home office. Cleaning services just for the office are fully deductible. If you take the flat rate ("safe harbor") Home Office deduction, cleaning services are included in the flat rate. See **Home Office**.
Clothing: Cleaning and laundry services for clothing used exclusively for work are deductible, but only if the clothing is unsuitable for street wear, such as a uniform, costume, or protective gear. Clothing with your company's logo or advertising is considered a uniform, and therefore deductible. Cleaning and laundry services for your regular clothing are deductible when traveling away from home overnight on business.
Expense category: Office expense. Travel (if traveling).

Clothing

Clothing used exclusively for work and unsuitable for street wear is deductible. Includes uniforms, costumes, and protective gear. Clothing with your company's logo or advertising is considered a uniform, and therefore deductible. Cost of cleaning is deductible.
Expense category: Supplies.

I have had difficulty recognizing the end of a work day. Eating dinner and then going back to work. Waking up early and heading directly for the computer. Maintaining the balance between work and the rest of our lives gets a little fuzzy when all of it takes place in the same location.

—Rosemarie Atencio, Health and Wellness Dynamics,
Veneta, Oregon

Cloud Computing

Cost of renting or leasing cloud software is deductible. See **Software**.

Clubs

Dues and other expenses for business groups, professional organizations, merchant and trade associations, chambers of commerce, etc. are deductible. Dues to community service organizations, such as Rotary, Lions, etc., are deductible.
Expense category: Other expenses.
If part of your dues to a trade or professional association are for political lobbying, that portion of the dues is not deductible.
Dues and membership fees in clubs run for pleasure, recreation, or other social purposes are not deductible. These include athletic, luncheon, hotel, airline, sporting and other entertainment or recreational organizations, associations, clubs, and facilities. Even if you use a club membership solely to generate or discuss business, the dues are not deductible. Sometimes the term "business club" is used to describe such a facility. If the "business" club is not a business organization, the dues are not deductible. Entertainment costs at these clubs, if for business, are 50 percent deductible. See **Entertainment**.

I love it whenever Congress passes tax changes. We grow and continue to expand.

—John Hewitt, founder and CEO, Liberty Tax Service

Collection Agency

Fees charged by collection agencies are deductible.
For businesses on the cash basis of accounting, accounts turned over to collection agencies that the agencies collect for you, should be added to income at the time the money comes in: the amount you actually receive, not the full amount owed you.

Accounts turned over to collection agencies that the agencies are unable to collect, can only be deducted if the amounts were already included in income, as explained under **Uncollectible Accounts**. Cash basis businesses do not get a deduction for these uncollectible accounts.

Expense category: Legal and professional services.

Commissions

Commissions paid to outside salespeople or companies, commissions paid for referrals, finder's fees, and the like are deductible.

Expense category: Commissions and fees. If you pay $600 or more in commissions in a calendar year to an individual, you are required to report those commissions to the IRS on Form 1099-MISC.

Commissions paid to acquire new customers who sign long-term contracts, may have to be capitalized and deducted over a period of years. The IRS says the deduction must be spread over the average number of years new customers stay with the business. This is something you should ask your accountant about.

A business broker's commission for helping to buy or sell a business may have to be amortized (deducted) over five years. See **Buying a Business**.

Community Service

Community service expenses are often deductible, depending on what you actually are spending money on. You should check with your accountant.

Expense category: Varies depending on actual expenses.

Commuting

Regular commuting expenses, home to your regular place of business and back, are not deductible. Any business travel other than commuting—to customers, to suppliers, or for any other business purposes—is deductible. See **Travel**.

Home business owners do not commute to work, but there is one fine point in the commute law. If you drive to visit clients, the IRS considers the trip to your first client a commute, not deductible. The same goes for the trip home from your last call of the day.

There may be a way to avoid this loss of a deduction. If you go to your home office and do some work before you visit your first client, most accountants feel that you already did your commute (to your home office), and that your first client visit is deductible. Ditto for returning home after visiting your last client, if you return to your home office to work before quitting for the day. Pretty picky rules here, I admit. Part of the secret to success in business is (1) knowing the rules, and (2) knowing how to break them.

Employers: Employers can pay up to $250 a month per employee for transit passes or employer-provided van pool vehicles and up to $20 a month to employees who bicycle to work. The payments are not taxable to the employees. (S corporation employees are eligible but not the S corporation owners themselves.)

Expense category: Employee benefit programs.

Compensation

Compensation to employees is deductible. Compensation paid to independent contractors and commissioned salespeople is deductible. Compensation to yourself is deductible only if you are an employee of your own corporation. See: **Payroll, Commissions, Draw.**

Expense category: Wages (for employees). Commissions and fees (for independent contractors, salespeople, other non-employees).

Computers

Computers and peripherals (monitors, printers, etc.) can be deducted or depreciated. See **Business Assets, Depreciation.** If the computer is used away from your business premises, the computer must be used more than 50 percent for business, or no deduction allowed.

Expense category: Depreciation (also fill out Form 4562, "Depreciation and Amortization").

Computer Programs

Computer programs can be deducted the year of purchase, with limitations, or depreciated over a period of years. Computer programs that are rented or subscribed to can be deducted currently. See **Software**.

Condominium

A condominium that houses your home office is part of the **Home Office** deduction. You can deduct the business portion of the rent if you rent your home, or the business portion of the depreciation if you own your home. Homeowners who depreciate the business part of their homes should be especially aware of tax problems that can come up when you sell the home. This is a very important issue, covered under **Home Office**. If you take the flat rate ("safe harbor") Home Office deduction, condo rent or depreciation is included in the flat rate.

See **Home Office**. Also see **Interest, Property Taxes**.

Conferences

Costs of conducting or attending business conferences are deductible. Travel (with a few exceptions) and lodging are deductible. Meals are 50 percent deductible. See **Travel, Meals**.

Expense category: Other expenses (for the conference itself). Travel.

Consignment

Consigned inventory is merchandise a business or self-employed individual places with another business for the other business to try to sell.

For example, a dress maker may consign inventory to a dress shop. The business consigning the goods (the dress maker) has not made a sale and does not get paid until the business that has taken the goods in on consignment (the dress shop) sells the goods.

For tax and inventory purposes, the consignor (in our example, the dress maker) has not sold the dress. There is no income to report. The dress should be included in the dress maker's year-end inventory. The consignee (the dress shop) has not purchased the dress until it re-sells the dress to its customer. The dress shop does not include the dress in its year-end inventory. See **Inventory**.

Expense category: Cost-of-goods-sold.

Bankruptcy and Consignment: Consignors should be warned that these consignment laws are income tax laws only. They may not hold up in bankruptcy court. If the dress shop files for bankruptcy before it sells the dress, the court can seize and sell consigned inventory to pay off the creditors of the dress shop, even though the shop doesn't legally own the goods. The dress maker will have to stand in line with all the other creditors hoping to get paid.

The dress maker can protect himself or herself by filing what's known as a UCC 1 (for Uniform Commercial Code) form with the county or state where the dress shop is located. This is a legal notice that the goods belong to the dress maker and not to the dress shop. It will usually hold up in bankruptcy court, enabling the consignor to get the unsold merchandise back.

If the dress was sold by the dress shop, but the shop filed for bankruptcy before paying the dress maker, the courts hold that this was a sale, that the dress maker is just another creditor who probably will never see her money. A UCC 1 filing will not help.

Construction Businesses

Some construction businesses are eligible for the Domestic Production Deduction, also known as the Manufacturer's Deduction. See **Manufacturer's Deduction**.

It's riskless. You can test it. If it tests no-go, you don't go.

—Doris Christopher, owner, The Pampered Chef

Consultants

Definition of a consultant #1: Someone who borrows your watch to tell you what time it is. Definition of a consultant #2: Someone who saves his client almost enough money to pay his fee.

Consultants' fees are deductible.

Expense category: Commissions and fees.

Containers

Boxes, cartons, and other containers and packaging materials that hold the goods you sell, are considered part of your inventory and included in cost-of-goods-sold. See **Inventory**. If, however, the cost of the containers or packaging is not significant or used only occasionally, most businesses deduct them as a current expense.

Expense category: Supplies.

Contract Labor

The term "contract labor" usually refers to **Independent Contractors**. Also see **Temporary Help Agency**.

Contractors

See **Independent Contractors**.

Contracts

The cost of preparing contracts is deductible. A payment to be released from a contract is deductible.

Expense category: Legal and professional services.

Contracts that are expensive to negotiate and prepare, and cover more than a year, must be amortized over the length of the contract. This is something you probably should discuss with your accountant.

Expense category: Depreciation. Also fill out Form 4562, "Depreciation and Amortization."

Contributions

Money you contribute to your own business is neither income nor expense, and is not deductible.

Also see **Charitable Contributions, Political Contributions**.

Conventions

The cost of attending a business convention in the United States is deductible. Travel and lodging expenses are deductible, meals are 50 percent deductible, entertainment is 50 percent deductible. The expense of a spouse traveling with you is not deductible unless the spouse is a partner or employee in the business and has a valid business reason for attending.

Conventions overseas may also be deductible, although the IRS has stricter rules. See **Travel**.

Expense category: Travel.

Copies

Deductible.

Expense category: Office supplies.

Copyrights

Copyrights and many other intangible assets are amortized (deducted) over a period of years. Copyrights are so inexpensive, however, that I would suggest that if you only have one or a few, write them off anyway. For more information on writing off assets over a period of years, see **Depreciation**.

Expense category: Taxes and licenses; or Depreciation (also fill out Form 4562, "Depreciation and Amortization").

Cost-of-Goods-Sold

Businesses cannot deduct the cost of inventory until the goods are sold. The expense is called "cost-of-goods-sold." See **Inventory**.
Expense category: Cost-of-goods-sold.

Costumes

Clothing used exclusively for work and unsuitable for street wear is deductible. This also includes uniforms and protective gear. Cost of cleaning is deductible.
Expense category: Supplies.

Courier Service

Any business service of this type is deductible.
Expense category: Office expense.

Covenant Not to Compete

See **Buying a Business**.

Credit and Debit Cards

Business purchases made with a credit card or debit card are fully deductible. You can use your personal credit or debit card for business purchases (sole proprietors only). You get a full business deduction for business purchases.

Credit and debit card fees and interest are also deductible. If the card is used partly for business, you prorate any bank charges or fees, personal vs. business. If you have interest charges, only the interest on business purchases can be deducted.

Taxes paid with credit or debit cards: Any card fees are deductible only for the business portion of the taxes.

Expense category: For purchases, category depends on what was purchased. For bank fees: Office expense. For interest charges: Interest.

Corporations: To maximize tax deductions and minimize paperwork, corporations should have credit and debit cards in the corporation's name, not in the owner's or employee's name. If you use your personal card to pay corporate bills, have the corporation reimburse you for your employee business expenses, to get the best tax advantage. See **Employee Business Expenses**.

Credits

If you receive a credit reducing the cost of something you are buying, treat the credit like a discounted price. The credit is not shown as a separate item on your ledgers or tax return.

Also see **Tax Credits**.

Customs

Customs fees, duties, and tariffs are deductible. Fees charged by customs brokers and international handlers are deductible. Instead of deducting customs fees immediately, in some cases the fees and duties can be added to the cost of inventory and written off as cost of goods sold. You may want to ask your accountant about this.

Expense category: Commissions and fees. Taxes and licenses.

Damaged Property

If business assets are damaged or destroyed, you are entitled to a deduction. See **Casualty Losses.** If inventory is damaged or destroyed, it can be deducted as part of cost-of-goods-sold. See **Inventory**.

Damages

Penalties for breach of contract are sometimes called damages. They are deductible.

Expense category: Other expenses.

Damage to business property is deductible. See **Casualty Losses**.

Damaged inventory is deductible as part of cost-of-goods-sold. See **Inventory**.

Also see **Punitive Damages**.

Day Care

Self-employed individuals cannot deduct the cost of day care for their own children, unless you are an employee of your own corporation. Employers can deduct day care expenses for their employees. See **Dependent Care**.

Day care business: Expenses for running a day care business are deductible like the expenses of any other business. If you run a day care business out of your home, see **Home Office** for special day care deductions allowed.

Debit Cards

See **Credit and Debit Cards**.

Decorating

Decorating expenses for the business are part of the **Home Office** deduction. If you take the flat rate ("safe harbor") Home Office deduction, decorating expenses are included in the flat rate. See **Home Office**.

Furniture is not considered a decorating cost or a Home Office expense, and is fully deductible. See **Furniture**.

Also see **Antiques, Art Treasures**.

Delivery Charges

If you pay delivery charges on goods you sell, the expenses are fully deductible.

Delivery charges on goods you receive are deductible, with two exceptions: Freight charges for inventory you are buying are included as part of the cost of the inventory. See **Inventory**. Freight charges for business assets you are buying (machinery, furniture, etc.) should be added to the cost of the asset. See **Business Assets**. However, if the amounts are minor, most businesses just deduct the delivery charges when paid.

Expense category: Other expenses.

Many women tell me, "I'd rather pay more taxes than risk an audit." I never hear it from men. This is clearly a problem.

—Jan Zobel, enrolled agent and tax advisor, Oakland, CA

Dependent Care

Dependent care (child care, day care) for your own family is not deductible as a business expense unless you are incorporated.

If you have employees, dependent care provided for your employees' families is deductible. You can also pay employees money for them to spend on dependent care, tax-free to the employees, up to $5,000 per year. You the employer get a deduction.

Employers can get a tax deduction to help employees who adopt children. Maximum deduction is $13,190.

Expense category: Employee benefit programs.

If you provide child care facilities for your employees, you may be eligible for an Employer's Child Care Tax Credit. See **Tax Credits**.

Dependent care business: If you operate a dependent care (day care) business out of your home, there are special office-in-home rules just for day care businesses. See **Home Office**.

Deposits

Refundable deposits are not deductible. Non-refundable deposits are deductible. Deposits that are actually prepayments of some expense come under the prepaid expense rules. See **Prepayments**.

Some deposits are called advances. An advance is really a prepayment for work to be done or goods to be delivered, not money you expect to get back. Advances are deductible. See **Advances**.

Expense category: Varies depending on actual expenses.

Depreciation

Depreciation is a tax term and means that the tax deduction for an asset is spread out over several years. When you depreciate an asset, you do not deduct the entire cost of the asset the year you purchase it. Each year, a portion of the cost is deducted. These assets are variously called fixed, capital, depreciable, or business assets.

Depreciable assets include buildings, components of buildings, vehicles, machinery, shop and office equipment, furniture, fixtures, tools, aircraft, boats, trailers, intangibles such as trademarks, patents and software, some farm animals, plants and trees. Major building improvements such as a new roof, and major repairs that extend the life of an asset, are treated as depreciable assets. Both new and used assets can be depreciated.

Depreciable assets do not include inventory, supplies, inexpensive tools, or anything that will not last more than a year. Generally, anything that costs $200 or less is written off when purchased, not depreciated.

Land cannot be depreciated or written off until sold, but some land improvements, including parking lots and landscaping, can be depreciated.

Home Office: If you own your home, the depreciation on the building is part of the **Home Office** deduction. Depreciation for the home is prorated, business versus personal, using the same percentage as the home office. Homeowners who depreciate the business part of their homes should be especially aware of tax problems that can come up when you sell the home. This is a very important issue, covered under **Home Office**. If you take the flat rate ("safe harbor") Home Office deduction, depreciation is included in the flat rate. See **Home Office**.

First-Year Write-Off

Depreciation can get quite complicated, that's the bad news. The good news is that, for many depreciable assets, depreciation can be avoided completely. Most assets other than buildings can be written off when purchased, up to certain dollar maximums. This "First-Year Write-Off" is covered under **Business Assets**.

The First-Year Write-Off is very easy to calculate, and depreciation is very difficult to calculate. So, why would anyone choose complex, multi-year depreciation over the simple, write-it-off-now deduction? Many new businesses make little or no profit the first year or two, and may not have any use for the additional tax savings the First-Year Write-Off deduction offers. It might be better to depreciate the assets, spreading the deduction over several years. In this way, you deduct the bulk of the expense in future years when you can use it to save taxes. You might want to calculate your profit and taxes under both methods to find the bigger tax savings.

Depreciation Methods

If you don't write off all of your assets the first year, you—or more likely your accountant—will have to calculate regular depreciation, a complicated procedure. The IRS has several depreciation methods to choose from, and several "write-off periods" or "recovery periods"— how many years you write off different assets. There are several categories of assets, each with a different write-off period. The categories most used by small businesses are:

3 Year Property: on-road tractor units, race horses over two years old, all horses over 12 years old, some software.

5 Year Property: vehicles; trailers; aircraft; most equipment used for research and experimentation; computers, copiers, fax machines, and similar office equipment; carpeting; movable partitions; outdoor signs and decorative lighting (building lighting is depreciated as part of the building); semi-conductor manufacturing equipment; solar, wind, and some other alternative energy property; some electronic equipment; some software; movable gasoline storage tanks; appliances, furniture, and rugs used in residential rental property.

7 Year Property: most machinery, equipment, furniture, fixtures, most signs; vending machines; railroad track; horses other than those listed as 3 year property.

10 Year Property: most boats (except pleasure craft, which are not deductible); barges and tugs; single-purpose agricultural and horticultural structures; fruit and nut trees and vines.

15 Year Property: gas stations, including their mini-marts (with some exceptions). Some golf course improvements. Parking lots. Major landscaping. Some intangible (intellectual) property such as goodwill, trademarks, trade names, franchises, customer lists, and covenants not to compete. Patents and copyrights are 15 year property only if acquired as part of a business you have purchased.

20 Year Property: all-purpose farm buildings.

27½ Year Property: residential rental buildings.

39 Year Property: all buildings other than those listed under 15 year, 20 year, and 27½ year property.

Other: Patents and copyrights are depreciated over the life granted by the government (except see 15 year property above).

Assets owned before going into business: Depreciable assets used in your business that were purchased before going into business can be depreciated regardless of when acquired. These assets are valued at their cost or at their market value at the time the assets are first used in your business, whichever is less. If some old machinery, or an old computer, which cost you $2,000 eight years ago, was only worth $500 (market value) when first used in your business, you may only depreciate $500.

Assets used partly for business: Depreciable assets used partly for business and partly for non-business can be depreciated to the extent used for business. For example, if you use your tools 50 percent for business and 50 percent for personal use, you can depreciate 50 percent of the cost.

Limitations on vehicles: Many, but not all, vehicles used for business have limitations on the maximum deductions you can take the first year and in subsequent years. Most heavy-duty trucks and vans, and some light-duty trucks are exempt from the limitations. Automobiles, some light-duty trucks, and many SUVs come under the limitations. Different vehicle categories have different limitations. Every year the IRS changes the limitation amounts, and even the vehicle categories subject to the limitations. Ever wonder what those IRS lawyers do in their spare time?

If you are considering purchasing a vehicle for business, I suggest you talk to your accountant before making a purchase, to find out if there is the possibility of a significant tax savings—or penalty—before making your purchase.

Selling assets. When you sell an asset, to figure profit or loss on the sale, the cost of the asset must be reduced by the "allowed or allowable" depreciation. This is an important tax law. The IRS figures the profit or loss on the sale of an asset as though you had taken depreciation, even if you didn't! If you fail to take depreciation or the first-year write-off, when you sell the asset, you lose coming and going: No deduction for depreciation (because you didn't take it), and no break when you sell the asset.

Worthless, abandoned, missing, or obsolete assets. If any assets you are depreciating are no longer working or useful, or are missing (missing?!), you can write off the entire undepreciated balance currently.

For full details, see IRS Publication 946, "How to Depreciate Property."

Expense category: Depreciation. Also fill out Form 4562, "Depreciation and Amortization."

Design Costs

Most design costs—brochures, packages, logos, etc.—are deductible. Cost of copyrighting or trademarking a design may have to be amortized; ask your accountant.

Expense category: Advertising.

Development

Product development expenses are usually deductible, and may also be eligible for special tax credits. See **Tax Credits**.

Some development cxpenses that will benefit future years may have to be capitalized, and deducted over a period of at least five years. You should discuss these expenses with your accountant.

Expense category: Other expenses.

Business development expenses may or may not be deductible, depending on whether you are just starting your business or already have an operating business. See **Start-Up Costs**.

Real estate developers: Pre-development costs such as planning and design, building permits, engineering studies, landscape plans, and the like, cannot be deducted currently, but must be capitalized. See **Buildings, Land, Renovations, Property Taxes, Restoration**.

Directors' Fees

Fees paid to corporate directors are deductible.

Expense category: Commissions and fees.

Disability Insurance

Disability insurance for your employees is deductible. Disability insurance for yourself is not deductible unless you are an employee of your own corporation. Insurance that pays for business overhead expenses during a time you are disabled is deductible.

Expense category: Employee benefit programs (for employees); Insurance (for Overhead Insurance).

Disabled Access

There are two tax deduction options for businesses that spend money to assist disabled customers and employees.

Businesses can take a Disabled Access Tax Deduction of up to $15,000 per year for architectural and transportation barrier removal. Costs in excess of $15,000 can be depreciated. If the expenses are for your home, they are part of the Home Office deduction. Your business must meet the IRS's Home Office requirements to deduct the cost. See **Home Office**.

There is also a Disabled Access Tax Credit of up to $5,000 a year, for architectural and transportation barrier removal, and also for acquiring or modifying equipment or devices for disabled individuals. Equipment and devices are not part of the home office, so this credit can be claimed in addition to home office expenses. Businesses that gross over $1 million or have over thirty employees are not eligible for this credit (but are eligible for the deduction). See **Tax Credits**.

Businesses can take either the "disabled access tax deduction" or the "disabled access tax credit," but not both on the same items. You can take the deduction on some assets, and the credit on other assets. Note that equipment and devices are not eligible for the disabled access tax deduction, but are eligible for the disabled access tax credit.

You may need the help of an accountant to figure out which option, or combination, will reduce your taxes the most.

Disaster Losses

Deductible, but with special rules. See **Casualty Losses**.

Discounts

"List price $1,599.00. On Sale Today $14.95."

Discounts given to customers and employees reduce your income. You show a lower gross income (sales) on your tax return. Discounts are not shown as an expense deduction.

You can give discounts to employees and their families for anything your business makes or sells, tax-free to them, as long as the discounted price is not below your cost.

Discounts on purchases reduce the cost of the items being purchased. Discounts should not be recorded or deducted separately.

Displays

Goods: Goods on display are considered inventory. See **Inventory**.
Fixtures: Display fixtures are business assets. See **Business Assets**.

Decorations: Display decorations can be deducted.
Expense category: Supplies.

Our hobby time turned out to be our market study and research rolled into one."

—Mayra Donnell, cofounder, Mayari Handmade Soaps, Maine

Dividends

Corporate dividends: When corporations distribute their profits to shareholders, these distributions are called dividends. Dividends are not considered business expenses and are not deductible.

How and when corporate profits are distributed, and how owners of corporations are compensated, can have a major impact on the taxes the corporation and the shareholders pay. I strongly recommend that you talk to an experienced accountant.

Any costs associated with distributing dividends, such as bank or broker fees, are deductible.
Expense category: Legal and professional services.

Dividend rebates: The word dividend has a second meaning unrelated to corporate profits. Rebates to customers are sometimes called dividends. These rebates are deductible.
Expense category: Returns and allowances.

Domain Name

Expenses associated with acquiring, registering, and keeping a domain name are deductible. Also see **Internet Access**.
Expense category: Other expenses.

Domestic Production Deduction

See **Manufacturer's Deduction**.

Donations

Only corporations can deduct charitable contributions and donations, although some businesses have been able to deduct charitable donations as advertising expenses. For more information, see **Charitable Contributions**.

Expense category: Charitable contributions.

Political donations are not deductible.

Downloads

Downloaded software is deductible. See **Software**.

Downloaded music and downloaded publications, if for your business, are deductible.

Expense category: Office expenses.

Draw

Draw, partner, refers to drawing money out of your business. When you are self-employed, as a sole proprietor, partner in a partnership, or member (owner) of a limited liability company, you are not an employee of your business. You do not get a salary or a wage. If you want some money from your business, you "draw" it; that is, you just take it. This is not an expense, this is not a tax deduction. It is not a taxable transaction. See **Paying Yourself.**

Corporations: If you own a corporation, the rules are very different. You do not "draw" money, but you do pay yourself a salary, taxable as regular employee wages. Any money you take out of a corporation in excess of your salary is also not a draw. It is a taxable dividend. See **Payroll, Dividends**.

Driveway

Costs of maintaining a private road or driveway are part of the **Home Office** deduction. Costs for the driveway are prorated, business versus personal, using the same percentage as the home office. If you take the flat rate ("safe harbor") Home Office deduction, costs related to a driveway are included in the flat rate.

See **Home Office**.

Drop Shipping

Drop shipping is a business arrangement where your business contracts with another business to warehouse and ship products to your customers for you. The drop shipper may be the manufacturer or importer or wholesaler of the products, selling the products to you but shipping them to your customers for you; or the drop shipper may simply be a warehouse and shipping service.

Goods that you have drop shipped for you are considered inventory even though you never have them in stock. You include the cost of the goods as part of your cost-of-goods-sold. See **Inventory**.

If the drop shipper charges you sales tax on the goods, the sales tax is considered part of the cost of the inventory. Any warehousing and shipping fees are deductible separately.

Dues

Dues for business groups, professional organizations, merchant and trade associations, chambers of commerce, etc. are deductible. Dues to community service organizations, such as Rotary, Lions, etc., are deductible.

Expense category: Other expenses.

Political: If part of your dues to a trade or professional association are for political lobbying, that portion of the dues is not deductible.

Clubs: Dues and membership fees in clubs run for pleasure, recreation, or other social purposes are not deductible. These include athletic, luncheon, hotel, airline, sporting and other entertainment or recreational organizations, associations, clubs, and facilities. Even if you use a club membership solely to generate or discuss business, the dues are not deductible. Sometimes the term "business club" is used to describe such a facility. If the "business" club is not a business organization, the dues are not deductible.

Duties

Customs fees, duties, and tariffs are deductible. Fees charged by customs brokers and international handlers are deductible. Instead of deducting customs duties immediately, in some cases the duties can be added to the cost of inventory and written off as cost-of-goods-sold. You may want to ask your accountant about this.

Expense category: Legal and professional services. Taxes and licenses.

Education Expenses

There are two different education deductions for businesses:

(1) The **Self-Employed Education Deduction** is for sole proprietors, partners, and members of limited liability companies. This deduction is for your own education. This deduction is not for corporations nor for your employees.

(2) If you have employees, the **Employer Paid Education for Employees** deduction is for your employees. If you own a corporation, you are an employee of your corporation, and are eligible for this deduction.

Self-Employed Education Deduction

The cost of education for self-employed individuals is deductible, if the education maintains or improves a skill required in your business. Education expenses are not allowed if the education is required to meet minimum educational requirements of your present business or if the education will qualify you for a new trade or business.

A self-employed welder who takes a course in a new welding method can charge the expense to the business. A self-employed dance teacher who also takes dance lessons can deduct the cost of the lessons. On the other hand, a store owner who takes a course to become a general contractor cannot deduct the expenses. The education must be directly related to the business you already operate. Taking a course in pottery before opening your pottery shop is not deductible. Any self-employed person can take a course in bookkeeping or taxes or computers and deduct the cost.

Expense category: Other expenses.

Employer-Paid Education for Employees

Job related education: Employers can deduct, and employees can exclude from their income, the cost of job-related education expenses. If you own your own corporation, you are an employee of the corporation, and this deduction applies to you.

Non-job related education: Employers can also pay up to $5,250 annually for employee education expenses that are not job related. The payments must be part of a written educational assistance program. If the education involves sports, games, or hobbies, the education must be job related. Payments in excess of the $5,250 are considered wages, subject to payroll taxes and income taxes. If you own your own corporation, non-job related payments for your own education may be limited; ask your accountant.

Expense category: Employee benefit programs. Wages.

Education expenses include tuition, course fees, books, laboratory fees, travel between your business and the class location, and travel expenses while away from home overnight. Overnight travel is subject to limitations. See **Travel**.

For more information, see IRS Publication 970, "Tax Benefits for Education."

Also see **Scholarships**.

Electricity

Home electricity expenses are part of the **Home Office** deduction. Home electricity costs are prorated, business versus personal, using the same percentage as the home office. If you take the flat rate ("safe harbor") Home Office deduction, home electricity expenses are included in the flat rate. See **Home Office**.

Solar electric: If you purchase a solar electric system, you may also be eligible for an Energy Tax Credit. See **Tax Credits**.

Electronics

Electronic equipment and devices are considered business assets, which can be depreciated or written off the year of purchase. See **Business Assets**.

Service contracts, extended warranties, and insurance policies can be deducted currently if they do not exceed 12 months. See **Prepayments**.

Employee Business Expenses (Employers)

If the employer reimburses an employee for out-of-pocket business expenses, the employer is entitled to a tax deduction for the expenses. However, there are some strict IRS rules about reimbursing employees, and how the reimbursements affect employee wages. See **Reimbursements**. This is an area the IRS is likely to examine if you are audited.

Remember that a self-employed individual—sole proprietor, partner, or owner of a limited liability company—is not an employee of the business. Employee business expense reimbursements do not apply to self-employed individuals. Owners of corporations are employees of their businesses.

Expense category: Varies depending on actual expenses.

Employees (Employers)

Wages and benefits you pay your employees are deductible. See **Payroll** and **Fringe Benefits**. If you employ your spouse, see **Spouse**. If you employ your children, see **Children on Payroll.** Also see **Paying Yourself**.

Expense category: Wages.

Leased employees: See **Temporary Help Agency**.

Employment Agencies (Employers)

Employment agency fees are deductible.

Expense category: Commissions and fees.

Also see **Temporary Help Agency.**

Sixty-one percent of self-employed individuals under-report their incomes.

—U.S. Government Accountability Office (GAO)

Employment Taxes (Employers)

Deductible. See **Payroll Taxes**.
Expense category: Taxes and licenses.

Energy

Home energy expenses are part of the **Home Office** deduction. Home energy costs are prorated, business versus personal, using the same percentage as the home office. If you take the flat rate ("safe harbor") Home Office deduction, home energy expenses are included in the flat rate. See **Home Office**.

Solar electric: If you purchase a solar electric system, you may also be eligible for an Energy Tax Credit. See **Tax Credits**.

Also, look up individual subjects.

Engineering Firms

Some engineering firms are eligible for the Domestic Production Deduction, also known as the Manufacturer's Deduction. See **Manufacturer's Deduction**.

Entertainment

Only 50 percent of entertainment expenses are deductible. To get the deduction, business must be conducted: not necessarily a transaction, but some discussion or other genuine business involvement is necessary. Keep a record of who you entertained, and what was discussed.

In some cases there is a fine line as to what is entertainment, subject to the 50 percent limit, and what is not entertainment and therefore fully deductible. For example, a fashion show put on by a dress designer would not be considered entertainment, but a 100 percent deductible business expense. A party or lunch after the show, however, would be entertainment subject to the 50 percent limit.

A business dinner or party in your home is also eligible for this 50 percent entertainment deduction. All businesses, not just home businesses, are eligible.

Some entertainment is 100 percent deductible. A company or holiday party where all employees are invited—and customers and prospective customers could also be invited—is 100 percent deductible. Travel to and from an entertainment event or facility, including parking, is 100 percent deductible.

If you are in the business of entertainment, the cost of entertainment provided to paying customers is 100 percent deductible.

The cost of owning or leasing an entertainment facility is not deductible.

Sometimes the term "promotion" is also called "entertainment." But promotion expenses are fully deductible, and entertainment is limited to a 50 percent deduction. You get to define your own expenses: the right choice of words will get you the right deduction.

Red Flag Audit Warning: Entertainment is more likely to get an IRS second look than other expenses. Don't classify an expense as entertainment unless it truly is. In fact, if entertainment expenses are not going to reduce your taxes much, consider not deducting them at all.

For more information, see IRS Publication 463, "Travel, Entertainment and Gift Expenses."

Expense category: Travel, meals, and entertainment.

Equipment

Equipment can be deducted or depreciated. See **Business Assets, Depreciation**.

Expense category: Depreciation.

Equipment, although it might be for the home office, is not considered part of the Home Office deduction and does not come under the Home Office rules. Equipment can be deducted in addition to the Home Office deduction.

Estimated Taxes

Sole proprietors, partners in partnerships, owners of limited liability companies (LLCs), and owners of S corporations are required to make quarterly prepayments of their federal income and self-employment taxes, if the combined taxes are $1,000 or more. The government wants your tax money, in advance, just like the taxes withheld from employee paychecks. Use Form 1040-ES.

C corporations make quarterly tax prepayments if estimated federal income tax for the year is $500 or more. File Form 1120-W.

These estimated tax payments are not deductible expenses.

Exchange

Exchange, as in trade or barter, is a taxable transaction. Goods and services received in trade are deductible just like goods and services purchased with cash. See **Barter**.

Expense category: Varies depending on actual expenses.

Excise Taxes

Federal excise taxes, if levied, are deductible. For more information, see IRS Publication 510, "Excise Taxes."

Some states call their corporate income tax an excise tax. Income taxes have different rules. See **Income Taxes**.

Expense category: Taxes and licenses.

Expense Accounts

Does anyone who owns his or her own business actually have an expense account? Expense accounts per se are not deductible, but the actual expenses are deductible, depending on what the expenses are actually for.

If you are an employee of your own corporation, see **Employee Business Expenses**.

Exporting

Customs fees, duties, and tariffs are deductible. Fees charged by customs brokers and international handlers are deductible.

Expense category: Commissions and fees. Taxes and licenses.

Exterminator Service

Exterminator services are part of the Home Office deduction. Costs for the entire home are prorated, business versus personal, using the same percentage as the home office. Service just for the office is fully deductible. If you take the flat rate ("safe harbor") Home Office deduction, the expenses are included in the flat rate. See **Home Office**.

Family

A spouse or a parent on your payroll is treated like any other employee, except a spouse and parents are not subject to Federal Unemployment (FUTA) tax (Unincorporated businesses only). See **Spouse**, **Parents on Payroll**.

Your own children on the payroll, if under the age of eighteen, may be exempt from income and payroll taxes. See **Children on Payroll**.

Expense category: Wages.

Fees

Some fees are deductible, and some fees may have to be amortized over several years. Look up the individual fees.

FICA Tax (Employers)

FICA stands for Federal Insurance Contributions Act. FICA tax is another name for the combined Medicare and Social Security payroll taxes deducted from every employee's paycheck and collected from every employer. Employer's portion is deductible. See **Social Security Tax**.

Expense category: Taxes and licenses.

Film and Video Producers

Some film and video producers are eligible for the Domestic Production Deduction, also known as the Manufacturer's Deduction. See **Manufacturer's Deduction**.

Finance Charges

Finance charges are usually deductible, but sometimes with restrictions. See **Interest**.
Expense category: Interest.

Finder's Fees

Finder's fees, commissions, and the like, are deductible.
Expense category: Commissions and fees.

Fines

Fines and penalties for violation of the law are not deductible. Penalties for not meeting contract requirements, and any other fines or penalties that do not involve breaking the law, are deductible.
Expense category: Other expenses.

Fire Protection Systems

Inexpensive fire protection equipment such as a fire extinguisher can be deducted.
Expense category: Office expense.
More elaborate fire protection systems are part of the **Home Office** deduction. Fire protection costs for the entire home are prorated, business versus personal, using the same percentage as the home office. Fire protection just for the office is fully deductible. If you take the flat rate ("safe harbor") Home Office deduction, the cost of a fire protection system is included in the flat rate. See **Home Office**.

First Aid

Medical supplies, emergency supplies, aspirin, etc. are fully deductible.
Expense category: Office expense.

First-Year Write-Off

Many assets purchased for your business can be deducted when purchased. See **Business Assets**.

Fixed Assets

Fixed assets are machinery, equipment, furniture, fixtures, and the like: assets the business owns, not for sale. They're staying, or fixed, as in fixed in place, not as in fixed a million times and they still don't work. Fixed assets are also known as capital assets, depreciable assets, and business assets. Some fixed assets are deductible the year purchased, and some must be depreciated. See **Business Assets, Depreciation**.

Fixed Costs

Fixed costs refer to overhead, the dozens of large and small expenses you pay whether you are generating income or not. Most fixed costs are deductible. See **Overhead**.
Expense category: Varies depending on actual expenses.

There is a big gap between what the IRS permits and what companies do in practice.

—U.S. Chamber of Commerce

Fixing-Up Expenses

Minor repairs and remodeling expenses are part of the **Home Office** deduction. Costs for the entire home are prorated, business versus personal, using the same percentage as the home office. Costs just for the office are fully deductible. If you take the flat rate ("safe harbor") Home Office deduction, fixing-up expenses are included in the flat rate. See **Home Office**.

Major repairs and renovation will have to be added to the cost of the home. See **Buildings**.

Fixtures

Built-in shop and building fixtures for your business are part of the Home Office deduction. Built-in fixtures that become part of a building may have to be depreciated along with the structure. If you take the flat rate ("safe harbor") Home Office deduction, fixtures are included in the flat rate. See **Home Office**.

Store fixtures in a store outside the home can be deducted or depreciated. See **Business Assets, Depreciation**.

Expense category: Depreciation.

Flexible Spending Accounts (Employers)

A flexible spending account is an employee fringe benefit plan. See **Cafeteria Plan**.

Floor Tax

This is actually a property tax on inventory, sometimes levied by local and state governments. Inventory sits on the floor, which is why the tax is sometimes called a floor tax. Inventory also sits on shelves, but the tax is never called a shelf tax. Whatever it is or isn't called, the tax is deductible.

Expense category: Taxes and licenses.

Flowers

Yes, flowers are deductible, for the office, for your secretary, for a customer or client, for an office party.

Expense category: Office expense.

Food

Food samples available to the public are fully deductible. Food and beverages served at business-related events, such as a demonstration or exhibit, are deductible.

Expense category: Cost-of-goods-sold (if samples); or Advertising.

Meals are partly deductible, if they meet certain IRS requirements. See **Meals**.

Businesses that sell food: Food is deducted as inventory. See **Inventory**.

Foreign Expenses

Payments to companies and individuals outside the United States, ("offshoring" expenses) come under the same laws as payments to U.S. companies. They are fully deductible if they meet the deduction requirements.

Expense category: Varies depending on actual expenses.

Foreign income taxes: If you pay income taxes to a foreign country, you may be eligible for a tax credit. See **Income Taxes, Tax Credits**.

Franchise Fees

Business franchise fees you pay to become a franchisee, licensee, distributor, etc., may have to be amortized (deducted) over a period of years. You should check with your accountant. Ongoing franchise fees are deductible.

Expense category: Commissions and fees.

Franchise taxes: Do not confuse franchise fees with franchise taxes. They are completely different. See **Franchise Taxes**.

Franchise Taxes

Franchise taxes are state taxes on corporations. Corporations are licensed by the states. Each state grants corporations what they call a franchise to do business in the state, for which they charge an annual franchise tax. Some franchise taxes are annual fees, some take the form of an income tax. They are deductible on your federal return.

Don't confuse this franchise tax with taxes on franchise businesses (McDonald's, Holiday Inn, those kinds of businesses). The word franchise has two different meanings here. All corporations, whether they are franchises or not, pay state franchise taxes.

Most states do not impose franchise taxes on unincorporated businesses. But if your unincorporated business does pay a state franchise tax, it is deductible if it is not an income tax. See **Income Taxes**.

Expense category: Taxes and licenses.

Fraud

If your business is defrauded, you may or may not be entitled to a tax deduction depending on what kind of fraud actually occurred. See **Theft Losses** and **Casualty Losses**.

Free Agents

Free agent is another term for independent contractor. Fees charged by free agents are deductible. See **Independent Contractors**.

Expense category: Commissions and fees.

If you are a free agent, you are in business for yourself and are entitled to all of the business deductions listed in this book.

Freelancers

Fees charged by freelancers and other independent professionals are deductible. See **Independent Contractors**.

Expense category: Commissions and fees.

If you are a freelancer, you are in business for yourself and are entitled to all of the business deductions listed in this book.

Freight

Freight refers to all shipping, handling, and delivery charges. Freight costs on goods you sell are fully deductible. Freight on goods you receive are deductible, with two exceptions:

Freight charges for inventory you are buying must be included as part of the cost of the inventory. See **Inventory**. Freight charges for business assets you are buying (machinery, furniture, etc.) should be added to the cost of the asset. See **Business Assets**.

Expense category: Other expenses.

Fringe Benefits (Employers)

Employers can deduct the cost of employee fringe benefits, with some exceptions and limits. Fringe benefits for you, the business owner, and your family may or may not be deductible depending on how your business is structured.

See **Awards, Business Gifts, Commuting, Dependent Care, Discounts, Education Expenses, Health Insurance, Life Insurance, Medical Expenses, Parking, Retirement Plans.**

See IRS Publication 15-A, "Employer's Supplemental Tax Guide."

Expense category: Employee benefit programs.

Fuel

Vehicles: Fuel for vehicles, aircraft, and boats is deductible. See **Vehicles**.

Expense category: Car and truck expenses. You may be eligible for a tax credit if you use alternative non-fossil fuels. See **Tax Credits**.

Home Office: Heating fuel and other utilities are part of the Home Office deduction. Costs for the entire home are prorated, business versus personal, using the same percentage as the home office. Costs just for the office is fully deductible. If you take the flat rate ("safe harbor") Home Office deduction, home fuel costs are included in the flat rate. See **Home Office**.

Furniture

Furniture can be deducted, with limits, or depreciated. See **Business Assets**. Furniture, although it is for the home office, is not considered part of the Home Office deduction and does not come under the Home Office rules. Furniture can be deducted in addition to the Home Office deduction.

Expense category: Depreciation.

Gambling Expenses

Generally, gambling expenses are not deductible as business expenses. However, if you take a prospective customer gambling, some accountants think this qualifies as an entertainment expense, if the gambling is legal. See **Entertainment**. In my opinion, claiming a deduction for gambling is just inviting an audit—and a lot of trouble.

Professional gamblers: Professional gamblers who are in the business of gambling can deduct gambling expenses as business deductions, just like any other business, as long as the gambling is legal in your state. Business deductions are not allowed for illegal activities.

However, be aware that the IRS is much more likely to examine a gambling-business tax return than one for a more conventional type of business. The IRS is very suspicious—often correctly—that the gambling is really a hobby, not a business. This is an area you may want to discuss with a tax accountant (hopefully not with your criminal defense attorney).

The more complex the rules, the harder it is for any of us to really know whether we're being hosed or catching a break. Any simplification of the tax code would make it harder for our legislators to be able to say to us that we personally are benefiting from their latest addition to the volume of tax rules. It's a great system for the IRS.

—Herbert W. Lovelace, columnist

Garbage Service

Garbage pickup costs and other utilities are part of the **Home Office** deduction. Costs for the entire home are prorated, business versus personal, using the same percentage as the home office. Costs just for the office are fully deductible. If you take the flat rate ("safe harbor") Home Office deduction, garbage fees are included in the flat rate. See **Home Office**.

Gardening Expenses

According to the IRS, landscaping and lawn care are not deductible for home-based businesses, even if done solely to enhance the image of the business. The only exception to this rule has been for home-based landscapers, if they are using the landscaping to demonstrate or advertise their services.

The Tax Courts have disagreed with the IRS on the landscaping deduction for home businesses and have allowed an allocatable share of landscaping and lawn care costs to be deducted, as part of the Home Office deduction, if the home business had clients visiting on a regular basis and the appearance of the residence and the grounds would be of significance to the business operations. You may want to ask your accountant about this.

If you do decide to deduct gardening expenses, they will be part of the Home Office deduction, prorated business versus personal. If you take the flat rate ("safe harbor") Home Office deduction, it doesn't matter whether gardening is deductible or not: all home-related expenses are included in the flat rate. See **Home Office**.

General Business Credit

This is not one, but several tax credits lumped under one heading. Tax credits are different than tax deductions, and can reduce your taxes significantly. Look up individual credits. Also see **Tax Credits**.

Expense category: Tax credits are taken on Form 1040.

Gifts

Gifts are deductible, with limits. See **Business Gifts**.
Expense category: Other expenses.

Goodwill

A successful business is worth more than a new business or a failing business, because satisfied customers will continue to patronize a successful business. That intangible "worth more" is called goodwill (also called "blue sky" or "going concern value"). A portion of the purchase price of a business is often allocated to goodwill. See **Buying a Business**.

Goodwill can be amortized (depreciated) over 15 years. See **Depreciation**.

Expense category: Depreciation. Also fill out Form 4562, "Depreciation and Amortization."

Graphic Design

See **Design Costs.**

Greeting Cards

Deductible. Good public relations, too. Send lots of greeting cards.
Expense category: Office expense.

Grooming

Personal grooming expenses are not deductible, except when traveling away from home overnight on business. See **Travel**. Grooming expenses related to a show or other promotion are deductible.

Expense category: Other expenses; or Travel (if traveling).

Gross Receipts Tax

A gross receipts tax is a tax on total business receipts—sales, income—before any deductions for expenses. The tax is in addition to any income or sales tax. Some states call their sales tax a gross receipts tax, but the tax referred to here is not a sales tax. Sales tax is collected from your customers. Gross receipts taxes are paid out of your own pocket.

Gross receipts taxes are deductible.

Expense category: Taxes and licenses.

Group Health Insurance

Generally, the cost of group health insurance plans for your employees is deductible. Former employees and families of employees can be included. Plans where you, the employer, reimburse employees for actual out-of-pocket medical expenses, are also allowed.

Expense category: Employee benefit programs.

Self-employed individuals: Group health insurance premiums for yourself come under different rules. See **Health Insurance**.

Guard Dog

There is no IRS ruling or code section spelling out what kind of deduction is allowed for a home-business watch dog. I suggest that businesses deduct this expense as part of the Home Office deduction, just like utilities and maintenance. See **Home Office**.

Gun

If having a gun is an ordinary and necessary expense of your business, it is deductible. See **Business Assets, Depreciation**.

Expense category: Depreciation. Also fill out Form 4562, "Depreciation and Amortization."

Handicapped Access

See **Disabled Access**.

Handling Charges

Handling and shipping charges are deductible, with some limitations. See **Freight**.
Expense category: Other expenses.

Health Benefits

See **Health Insurance** and **Medical Expenses**.

Health Insurance

Sole proprietors, partners in partnerships, members of LLCs, and owners of S corporations can deduct the full cost of health insurance for themselves, spouses, and dependents. The deduction, however, may not exceed the net profit from your business.

To get the health insurance deduction, the IRS says that the insurance plan must be either in the name of the business or in the name of the self-employed individual. If your spouse is shown as the main insured on your policy, ask your insurance company to change the name on the policy. The change should not affect your coverage or premiums.

I also suggest you pay the health insurance premiums from the business bank account, even if the policy is not in the business name. Some tax experts have stated that this is an IRS requirement. I've never found this requirement in the IRS code or any IRS notices or publications, but it certainly will help in the unlikely chance that an IRS auditor might challenge the deduction.

The health insurance deduction is not considered a business expense, does not reduce your business profit, and is not included on the business tax return. The deduction is taken on your 1040 return.

The deduction does not apply when computing self-employment tax. You pay self-employment tax on your net profit before taking the health insurance deduction.

The deduction is not allowed if you are eligible for employer-paid health insurance through your own employer (if you have another job) or through your spouse's employer.

Expense category: Not shown as a deduction on the business tax return. Deducted on the first page of the 1040 return.

Long-term care insurance: Premiums for long-term care insurance can be included as part of the above health insurance deduction. Long-term care insurance, however, is subject to a dollar limitation, which the IRS changes from year to year, and which varies depending on your age. The age and amount tables can be found in IRS Publication 535, "Business Expenses." There is no dollar limitation on regular health insurance.

Disability insurance that pays you for lost earnings if you are disabled, is not considered health insurance and is not deductible.

Medicare premiums for business owners (that is, the insurance premiums you pay when you are on Medicare) are deductible under the same rules as health insurance. Medicare premiums for spouses may or may not be deductible. The IRS has issued contradictory rulings on this issue. I suggest you check with an accountant.

Employee health insurance: Health and long-term-care insurance for your employees, their spouses, and dependents, are 100 percent deductible, as a business expense. The limitations for sole proprietors, partners, and owners of LLCs and S corporations (explained above) do not apply to employer-paid health insurance for employees.

In addition to the deduction, employers with 25 or fewer full time workers may also be eligible for a health coverage tax credit, to offset the cost of providing health insurance to your employees.

Employers can also reimburse employees for actual medical expenses (doctor bills, hospitals, prescriptions, lab tests, etc.) for the employees and employees' families. The employer gets a full deduction, and the payments are not taxable to the employees. These reimbursements are sometimes called a Cafeteria Plan, Flexible Spending Account (FSA), or Health Reimbursement Arrangement (HRA). This is something to discuss with an accountant.

Be careful not to reimburse employees for the cost of health insurance they themselves pay; the reimbursement may be considered taxable wages.

Expense category: Employee benefit programs.

Employers with 25 or fewer employees are eligible for a tax credit to offset the cost of employee health insurance. See **Tax Credits**.

Affordable Care Act ("Obamacare"): Costs for insurance required by the Affordable Care Act arc deductible like any other health insurance costs. Penalties for not purchasing insurance are not deductible.

Spouse on payroll: If your spouse is an employee of your business, on the payroll with regular employee payroll deductions, your spouse *and* family (i.e., you and your children) are eligible for full employee health benefits, and the cost is fully deductible as a business expense. You come under the "employee health insurance" rules, not the self-employed insurance rules. To get this deduction, all of your employees, if you have other employees, must be covered. Also, according to a recent IRS court case, the spouse must be the primary insured on the policy, and premiums must be paid from the business checking account.

C corporations: If you are an employee of your own C corporation (not an S corporation), you, your spouse, and dependents are eligible for full employee medical coverage, but only if all of your employees are covered. You cannot get a deduction for yourself if you do not include your employees.

S corporations: Owners of S corporations come under the same rules are sole proprietors and partners in partnerships. The owner of an S corporation can purchase health insurance and get a deduction on the owner's 1040 tax return.

As an alternative, the S corporation itself can purchase health insurance for the owner, or reimburse the owner for the cost of health insurance, and get a deduction for the insurance on the S corporation's tax return. But the S corporation must add the cost of the insurance to the owner's wages; the owner will be subject to income taxes the same as if the owner had been paid the money, except the additional "wage" (the cost of the health insurance) is not subject to Social Security-Medicare tax. This law applies only to owners of S corporations, not to employees who are not owners. Complicated enough for you?

Health Savings Accounts: If you have a high-deductible health insurance policy, you can set up and make tax-deductible contributions to a Health Savings Account (HSA). You can withdraw money from the account, tax free, to pay medical bills. You can set up an HSA just for yourself, or for your employees as well. Ask your bank or insurance company for details.

Also see **Medical Expenses**.

Work is something you do, not a place you go to.

—Woody Leonhart, author

Heating

Heating expenses are part of the Home Office deduction. Costs for the entire home are prorated, business versus personal, using the same percentage as the home office. Heating just for the office is fully deductible. If you take the flat rate ("safe harbor") Home Office deduction, heating expenses are included in the flat rate. See **Home Office**.

Hobbies

No deductions are allowed for hobbies unless your hobby is earning you a little money. Any profits from your hobby are taxable just like the profits from a business. Expenses of your hobby are deductible, but only up to the amount of income. In other words, you can show a profit (and pay taxes), or break even (and pay no taxes), but you cannot declare a loss. A business that is a real business and not a hobby can show a loss and be able to use that loss to offset other income in figuring your taxes.

When is an endeavor a hobby, and when is it a business? The IRS has a 3-year/5-year formula: if you do not show a profit for at least 3 out of 5 consecutive years, the IRS can declare your "business" to be a hobby and disallow any losses. This is not a firm rule, however. A business can deduct losses for several years in a row without being challenged by the IRS. In the event of an audit, the IRS will allow the ongoing losses if they are convinced that you are operating a real business and trying, though unsuccessfully, to make a profit.

The key issue is *intent*. What are you really doing? Trying to earn some money or just having fun? It will help if your business looks like a business—licenses, ledgers, bank account, business cards, etc.—and if you're devoting time to it in a businesslike manner.

Home Office

The term "home office," for this important tax law, refers to any home business space—office, workshop, studio, warehouse, store, showroom, etc.—and the expenses directly related to the space including rent or depreciation, utilities, insurance, mortgage interest, property taxes, home repairs, painting and decorating, alarm systems, air conditioning, etc.

The term "home" includes a house, apartment, loft, condominium, trailer, mobile home, or boat if you are living on it. The term also includes any separate structure that is part of your residence such as a garage, shop, or other building.

Failure to qualify for the home office deduction doesn't prohibit you from operating your business out of your home. It only means that the office itself, and all expenses directly related to the office space, are not deductible on your federal income taxes. You can still deduct all legitimate business expenses other than those directly related to the business space itself.

The home office rules apply to sole proprietors, partners in partnerships, and owners of LLCs. Partnerships and LLCs (the businesses themselves, not the owners) and corporations come under different rules, covered below.

To be eligible for the home office deduction, your business must meet two basic rules: (1) regular and exclusive use, and (2) principal place of business.

Rule 1: Regular and Exclusive Use

To be eligible for the home office deduction, a specific part of your home must be used regularly and exclusively for business. It can be a separate room or even part of a room as long as it is used for the business and nothing else. Period. No television in the office. No personal paperwork at the desk. (No games on the computer?) The business area can't double as a guest room, kid's room, or anything else, even when you are not working.

There are two exceptions to the exclusive rule: (1) If your home is your sole fixed location for a retail sales business and if you regularly store your inventory or your samples in your home, the expense of maintaining the storage area is deductible even if it isn't exclusive use of the space. (2) If you operate a licensed day care facility in your home, you do not have to use the space exclusively for business.

Rule 2: Principal Place of Business

In order for your home office to be deductible, it must meet at least one of these three requirements, in addition to the "regular" and "exclusive use" requirements above:

1. Your home office must be your principal place of business, defined by the IRS as "the most important, consequential, or influential location," with the main emphasis on where you meet with customers or clients. A second, less important criterion is where you spend the most time.
2. The home office must be used regularly (not just occasionally) by customers, clients, or patients, or to generate sales.
3. The home office must be the sole fixed location where you conduct substantial administrative or management activities for the business: where you do your paperwork, or your research, or ordering supplies, or scheduling appointments. You don't have to do all of your administrative or management work at home. The great bulk of it must be done at home and nowhere else.

Meeting any one of the three above requirements qualifies you for a home office deduction (as long as you also meet the Regular and Exclusive Use test).

If your business is also operated out of another location such as a store, you are still eligible for a home office deduction, in addition to the cost of renting the store, if the home office meets the above requirements.

You can have a separate "principal place of business" for each trade or business you operate.

Taking the Home Office Deduction

There are two options for taking a home office deduction: (1) you can take a standard flat-rate deduction, or (2) you can deduct actual expenses.

Deducting actual expenses involves keeping detailed records of expenses, making multiple calculations, filing Form 8829 "Expenses for Business Use of Your Home," and—if your home office is in a home that you own—possible tax problems when you sell the home.

The standard flat-rate deduction (the IRS calls it the "safe harbor method") is simple to figure, does not require Form 8829, and eliminates any home office tax complications when you sell your home.

You can calculate the home office deduction both ways and then decide which will give you the biggest deduction and the fewest hassles. Once you select a method, you are not stuck with it for future years. You can use one method one year, and the other method the next year if you want.

Option 1: Flat Rate (Safe Harbor) Deduction

The deduction is $5 per square foot of office space, up to a maximum of 300 square feet. So the maximum annual flat-rate deduction is $1,500. This flat-rate option is in lieu of deducting actual expenses for the space itself: rent or depreciation, insurance, property taxes, utilities, repairs, remodeling, maintenance. Office furniture and equipment, as well as all other normal business expenses other than those directly related to the office space, are deductible in addition to the flat rate.

The flat-rate deduction cannot exceed the net profit from the business. You can take the flat-rate deduction only up to the point your profit drops to zero. If your business is already showing a loss, you cannot take the deduction at all. Any unused part of the deduction cannot be applied to future years. The actual-expense deduction, by comparison, *can* be carried forward to future years. This is covered below.

Part-year business: If you operate a business for only part of a year—if you start or close the business during the year, or if you operate a seasonal business—you prorate the deduction for how many months of the year the business is in operation. Any month that you operate a business for 15 or more days can be counted as a full month in making the proration.

More than one business: If you have more than one business, the 300 square foot maximum is for all businesses combined. If a spouse or housemate also has a business, that person is also entitled to a $5 deduction for up to 300 square feet, but not for the same portion of the home. If two people share the same office space, the combined deduction cannot be more than the $5 per square foot.

Property taxes and mortgage interest: If you take the flat-rate deduction, you can still deduct property taxes and mortgage interest on Schedule A of your personal 1040 return if you itemize deductions.

Option 2: Deducting Actual Expenses

If you choose this option, deductible home office expenses include a percentage of your rent if you rent your home, or a percentage of the depreciation if you own your home, and an equal percentage of home utilities, property tax, building maintenance and repairs, mortgage interest and insurance. You can determine the percentage based on any reasonable allocation. Most people use either square footage or number of rooms in the house.

Landscaping and lawn care: According to the IRS, landscaping and lawn care are not deductible for home-based businesses, even if done solely to enhance the image of the business. The only exception to this rule has been for home-based landscapers, if they are using the landscaping to demonstrate or advertise their services. The Tax Courts have disagreed with the IRS on the landscaping deduction for home businesses and have allowed landscaping costs to be deducted. You may want to ask your accountant about this. (This is not an issue if you take the flat-rate deduction.)

Business loss: If your home business shows a loss, part of your home office expenses are not deductible this year. You may deduct all of your regular business expenses (other than expenses for the office space itself) and may deduct interest and property taxes on the office, regardless of profit or loss. But the remaining home office expenses may be deducted this year only if your business shows a profit. Any expenses you cannot deduct due to this limitation can be carried forward to the next year, and future years if the next year's income is not sufficient, and deducted then, again only up to the point where they do not create a loss next year.

Tax trap for homeowners: If you are eligible for the home office deduction, you will run into tax complications when you sell your house. Any depreciation you were allowed must be "recaptured." This means that you add up all the depreciation during all the years you had a home office, and pay tax on that depreciation when you sell the house. The additional tax, however, which you don't have to pay until you sell the house, is more than offset by the current tax savings (in both income and self-employment tax) if you take the deduction.

Another warning: If your home business is located in a separate structure on the same property—such as a detached garage, barn, even a structure specially built to house your business—when you sell your home, this structure is not eligible for the tax exemption homeowners get when they sell their homes. Any profit on the sale of the separate business structure is taxable. This is in addition to any tax on depreciation recapture. This quirk in the law applies only to separate structures, not to a home business located inside your main residence or in an attached garage.

These two warnings to homeowners only apply if you are deducting actual expenses. If you take the flat rate "safe harbor" deduction, you don't have to calculate depreciation recapture or lower homeowners' tax exemptions.

If you own your home, talk to your tax accountant when you first start your home business. Find out if it will be to your advantage to claim a home office deduction.

Special Situations

Partnerships and LLCs: You are allowed a home office deduction only if the partnership or LLC Agreement requires you to have a home office and pay the costs. If your current Agreement does not include such a statement, amend the agreement to include this requirement. Also see "Other Options" below.

Corporations: If you own a corporation and work out of your home, your corporation does not get a home office deduction. You, as an employee of your corporation, can take a personal tax deduction as an employee business expense, if you are eligible and if you itemize deductions on Schedule A of your 1040 return.

Other Options for Partnerships, LLCs, and Corporations: Instead of taking the home office deduction on your personal tax return, you can have your partnership, LLC, or corporation reimburse you for the cost of your home office. The business itself then gets to take the deduction. The IRS requires that you have a written "accountable reimbursement plan" in order to get the deduction. You probably need the help of an accountant to set up this plan.

One option to avoid is leasing your home office to your business. While this gives your business a legitimate deduction, it saddles you with taxable rental income and a possible loss of your home tax exemptions.

Child care and day care businesses: The home deduction is allowed only if your business is officially licensed as a child care or day care business (unless your business is exempt from state licensing rules) and your business cares for children, people age 65 or older, or people who are unable to care for themselves. If a room or rooms, or the entire house, is used for day care each business day, the IRS considers it used for the entire day. No need to prorate it for hours of use. Licensed child and day care businesses are also exempt from the exclusive use rule. You get a full deduction for rooms used in your business even if they are also used for non-business purposes.

Lodging Businesses: If you operate a separate hotel or inn on your property, it is not considered a home business. You do not have to meet the home-office rules. If you operate a bed and breakfast, boarding house or rooming house in your home, only the portion of the home used exclusively for the business can be deducted. Shared space (combined personal and lodging) and your private space cannot be deducted. However, you could have an office in your private space and get a deduction for the office in addition to the deduction for the lodging space.

Expense Categories

Sole Proprietors: A sole proprietor takes the home office deduction on Schedule C. Sole proprietors also fill out Form 8829, "Expenses for Business Use of Your Home." Note that you do not report home office depreciation, utilities, property taxes, or other home office expenses on the expense categories normally used for these deductions. All home office expenses are reported on Form 8829.

Partnerships: If you are a partner in a partnership or an owner (member) of an LLC, the deduction goes on Schedule E of your personal 1040 tax return.

Corporations: If you own a corporation, the deduction goes under Employee Business Expenses on Schedule A of your personal 1040 return. If your business reimburses you for the cost of your home office (covered above), the deduction goes on the business tax return, not on your personal tax return.

For more information, see IRS Publication 587, "Business Use of Your Home."

Homeowner's Fees/Associations

Homeowner's fees are part of the **Home Office** deduction. Homeowner's fee are prorated, business versus personal, using the same percentage as the home office. Any fees just for the business are 100 percent deductible. If you take the flat rate ("safe harbor") Home Office deduction, the fees are included in the flat rate. See **Home Office**.

HR 10 Plan

Another name for a Keogh tax-deferred retirement plan. See **Retirement Plans**.

Expense category: Deducted on the 1040 form.

Husband on Payroll

See **Spouse**.

Illegal Expenses

Not all outlaws are criminals, but it's illegal to take a deduction for illegal expenses. Just say no deduction allowed.

Importing

Customs fees, duties, and tariffs are deductible. Fees charged by customs brokers and international handlers are deductible. Instead of deducting customs fees immediately, in some cases the fees and duties can be added to the cost of inventory and written off as cost-of-goods-sold. You may want to ask your accountant about this.

Expense category: Taxes and licenses. Commissions and fees.

Improvements

Home improvements are part of the **Home Office** deduction. Home improvement costs for the entire home are prorated, business versus personal, using the same percentage as the home office. Improvement costs just for the office are fully deductible. Major home improvements may have to be added to the cost of the building and depreciated as part of the building. If you take the flat rate ("safe harbor") Home Office deduction, home improvement expenses are included in the flat rate. See **Home Office**.

Incentives

Incentive payments to customers, vendors, and other non-employees are deductible, within limits. See **Awards**.

Expense category: Advertising, or Other Expenses.

Incentive payments to employees, other than token non-monetary gifts, are usually considered wages, taxable to the employee and subject to regular payroll taxes. However, employees can receive "employee achievement awards" that are not considered taxable wages. See **Awards**.

Income Taxes

Federal income taxes are not deductible.

Corporations can deduct state and local income taxes on their federal returns—if the taxes are levied on the business itself, not on the owner. Sole proprietorships, partnerships, and LLCs cannot deduct income taxes. See **State Taxes**.

Some states allow a deduction for federal income taxes on state income tax returns.

Expense category: Taxes and licenses.

Taxes paid with credit or debit cards: Any card fees are deductible only for the business portion of the taxes.

Foreign income taxes: If you pay taxes to a foreign country, you may be eligible for a special tax credit. See **Tax Credits**.

Incorporation Fees

Some start-up corporate fees may have to be capitalized or deducted over a period of years. See **Organizational Costs**. Any fees, licenses, etc. after start-up are fully deductible.

Expense category: Taxes and licenses.

Independent Contractors

Independent contractors (outside contractors) are people who sell their services to other businesses on a contract basis, usually for a temporary time or for a specific project. Independent contractors are really in business for themselves, just like any other individually owned business providing a service. Most freelancers, consultants, free agents, and self-employed professionals are independent contractors.

Independent contractors are not employees. You do not withhold taxes, pay employment taxes, or file payroll tax returns. When you hire an independent contractor, you pay the contractor his or her fee in full. The fee is fully deductible.

Accountants, the IRS, and the Tax Courts have been arguing for years over who should be classified as an employee and who should be classified as an independent contractor. Entire books have been written on the independent contractor vs. employee controversy. There are serious risks to businesses that misclassify employees as independent contractors, and significant costs may be at stake. If you are unsure how to classify a worker, get advice from an accountant.

Expense category: Contract labor.

I haven't paid taxes in years, one of the reasons I believe every-one should run a business.

—Shirley A., magazine publisher, New Jersey

Individual Retirement Arrangement

Better known as an IRA, this is a tax deferred retirement plan. See **Retirement Plans**.

Expense category: Deducted on the 1040 form.

Installment Purchases

When you buy anything in installments ("on time"), your deduction depends on what it is you are buying, and the accounting method you are using.

If you are buying depreciable business assets such as equipment, vehicles, furniture, fixtures, machinery, etc., you can start depreciating the full cost, or if the assets are eligible for the First-Year Write-Off, you can write off the full cost of the assets, even though you haven't paid for them. This is allowed even if you are on the cash method of accounting. See **Business Assets, Depreciation**.

If you are buying inventory, you cannot write off the inventory cost until you sell the inventory. See **Inventory**.

If you are buying anything other than depreciable assets or inventory, the deduction depends on the accounting method you are using. Cash method taxpayers deduct the payments as they are made. Accrual method taxpayers deduct the entire purchase price when the purchase is made; as payments are made, they are not deducted a second time. Any interest or finance charges can be deducted separately.

If you don't know what the last paragraph is talking about, I'd like to take this opportunity (this second opportunity, actually) to recommend a book I wrote called *Small Time Operator: How to Start Your*

Own Business, Keep Your Books, Pay Your Taxes, and Stay Out of Trouble. It will answer all your questions.

Insurance

Most business-related insurance premiums are deductible.

Expense category: Insurance.

Homeowners Insurance costs are part of the **Home Office** deduction. Costs for the entire home are prorated, business versus personal, using the same percentage as the home office. Insurance just for the office is fully deductible. If you take the flat rate ("safe harbor") Home Office deduction, the cost is included in the flat rate. See **Home Office**. If the homeowners' insurance includes extra coverage for business assets or liability (other than the office itself), the additional coverage is fully deductible in addition to the home office coverage.

Prepaid Insurance: Prepaid insurance, if it does not extend beyond twelve months, is deductible. Prepaid insurance beyond twelve months is prorated between years.

Special rules for certain types of insurance:

Vehicle insurance: Deductible only if you don't take the Standard Mileage Allowance. See **Vehicles**.

Workers' compensation insurance: Deductible for your employees. For self-employed individuals, workers' comp premiums for yourself are deductible only if your state requires you to cover yourself. If your own coverage is not required by state law, it is not deductible.

Disability insurance: Disability insurance for your employees is deductible. Disability insurance for yourself is not deductible unless you are an employee of your corporation.

Life insurance: Self-employed individuals cannot deduct the cost of life insurance on themselves. Premiums for group term life insurance paid by an employer on behalf of employees are deductible, but only if the employer is not a beneficiary. If coverage exceeds $50,000, the premiums must be included in the employee's compensation as additional wages, subject to payroll taxes.

Business interruption insurance: May or may not be deductible, depending on what the insurance actually covers. You should check with your accountant on the deductibility of this kind of insurance, as the tax law gets a bit confusing.

Self-insurance: Some businesses, in lieu of buying insurance, set aside funds to cover possible losses such as fire or theft or a liability claim against the business. Some people call these funds a "reserve." The money set aside or in the reserve is not considered a business expense and is not tax deductible.

Health insurance: Health insurance has so many rules, it has its own category. See **Health Insurance**.

Intangibles

Intangibles (also called intellectual property) are business assets you cannot see, such as copyrights, trademarks, patents, goodwill. Most intangibles are amortized (depreciated) over a period of years.

Software is considered an intangible, but it can be written off when purchased. See **Business Assets**. Some trademark expenses can be written off when paid. See **Trademark**.

Also see **Copyrights, Goodwill, Patents, Software**. For more on writing off assets over a period of years, see **Depreciation**.

Expense category: Depreciation. Also fill out Form 4562, "Depreciation and Amortization."

Intellectual Property

This is another term for intangibles, assets you cannot see such as goodwill, patents, trademarks and copyrights. See **Intangibles**.

Expense category: Depreciation. Also fill out Form 4562, "Depreciation and Amortization."

Interest Expense

Interest paid on business debts, interest on credit card purchases, and interest on purchases of business assets are deductible, with a few important exceptions.

Interest on back taxes is not deductible (except for corporations), even if the back taxes are business related.

Interest on a personal loan is deductible as a business expense if the loan was used for your business. Be sure to keep good records showing that the money was really put into your business.

On some equipment loans, you have the option to capitalize the interest (add it to the cost of the equipment) and deduct it over a period of years rather than deduct it currently. This may be advantageous to you if you are just starting out in business, are not making much money, and do not need the immediate deduction. I suggest you discuss this with your accountant.

Expense category: Interest.

Home loans: Interest on a home loan is part of the **Home Office** deduction. Interest is prorated, business versus personal, using the same percentage as the home office. If you take the flat rate ("safe harbor") Home Office deduction, home loan interest is included in the flat rate. See **Home Office**. Home loan interest can also be deducted on Schedule A of your personal 1040 return if you itemize expenses.

Prepaid interest: The IRS says that prepaid interest is not deductible until the year it applies to. Some tax courts disagree. You may want to ask your accountant about this.

Buying a business: If you borrow money to purchase part or all of an existing business, the laws can get complicated. Part of the interest may be deductible as a current business expense, but part may have to be capitalized. You will probably need an accountant's help.

Corporations: How you structure corporate finances can have a major effect on how much you pay in taxes. If you are an employee of your own corporation, and you get a personal loan to purchase business assets, the interest is not deductible as a business expense. If the corporation itself borrows the money, the interest is deductible.

Internet Access

The cost of internet access is fully deductible if used only for business. If used partly for business, you prorate the cost and deduct only the business portion.

Also see **Domain Name, Website**.

Expense category: Office expense.

Inventory

Inventory is merchandise—goods, products, parts—held for sale in the normal course of business. Inventory also includes repair shop parts and manufacturing parts, "raw materials" and supplies that will go into the making of a finished product, and work in process (partly finished goods you are making). Display items are considered inventory if you plan to eventually sell them. Samples you give away are considered inventory.

Not all of your inventory purchases can be deducted as current year expenses. Only the cost of those goods actually sold is deductible. This is called "cost-of-goods-sold." There is a very important distinction between inventory and cost-of-goods-sold; you should understand it completely. The cost of inventory unsold at year-end is an asset owned by you and will not be a deductible expense until sold (or until it becomes worthless; covered below).

Cost-of-goods-sold is your most important and usually your largest item of expense. The federal income tax form has two main categories of expense: (1) cost-of-goods-sold, and (2) all other. You will be required to show on your tax return how you calculated your cost-of-goods-sold.

Cost-of-Goods-Sold

Calculating cost-of-goods-sold is a three-step procedure:

Step 1: You start with the cost of your inventory on hand at the beginning of the year.

Step 2: You add all the inventory purchases during the year. Beginning inventory (from Step One), plus your purchases during the year, gives you the total inventory available for sale during the year.

Step 3: Subtract the ending inventory (the cost of inventory still on hand at the end of the year). The resulting figure is your cost-of-goods-sold: Inventory at January 1, plus purchases during the year, minus inventory on hand December 31, equals cost-of-goods-sold.

With me so far? If not, stop and go back. There aren't too many tax laws that require your full understanding, but this is one of them.

Inventory on Hand at Start of Business

If you are starting a new business and already have inventory on hand that you will be putting into the business, inventory you purchased before going into business, you can add the cost of that inventory (or the market value if less than cost) to the current year's purchases—even though you didn't buy it this year—and include it in your inventory for computing the cost-of-goods-sold.

Taking Inventory

At the end of the year you will need to make a list of inventory on hand. This is called "taking inventory" or "taking a physical inventory." (The word "inventory" refers to both the goods and to the procedure of counting the goods.) Inventory on hand at year end is usually valued at its cost to you and not at its sales price.

If for any reason your year-end inventory is worth less than what you paid, the inventory should be valued at this lesser amount. "Worth" refers to its retail value, what you can sell it for. If year-end inventory is totally worthless, it should be valued at zero. This inventory valuation method is known as "lower of cost or market": You value your year-end inventory at its cost or at its market value, whichever is less. You may have figured out that reducing the value (writing down) of your year-end inventory increases your cost-of-goods-sold expense, thereby decreasing your profits and your taxes.

If you do value your inventory at less than its cost, the IRS expects you to offer the devalued inventory for sale at the lower-than-market price, either before year end or within thirty days after the year end. You don't have to actually sell the inventory, but you do need to offer it for sale. If you have worthless inventory, some accountants interpret IRS law as requiring you to dispose of the inventory in order to get the deduction. You might want to ask your accountant.

Inventory Lost, Stolen, or Given Away

The cost of stolen or missing inventory and the cost of samples given away are deductible as part of cost-of-goods-sold. This missing inventory is not on hand at year end, so it is not included in your year-end inventory count. It automatically becomes part of your cost-of-goods-sold (even though it really wasn't sold—the term "cost-of-goods-sold" really should be "cost of goods sold, lost, stolen, given away, damaged, unsalable, etc."). No additional write-off is allowed.

Manufacturers and Crafts Businesses

Computing the cost of your inventory will be a difficult task, for two reasons. First, you calculate the cost not only of your raw materials but of your finished and partially finished goods as well. Value your inventory at its cost to you. That cost includes materials and paid labor. It does not include your own labor (unless you are an employee of your own corporation).

The other complication in computing cost-of-goods-sold is a nasty law called the Uniform Capitalization Rule. The rule applies to all manufacturers and other businesses that, to quote the IRS, "construct, build, install, manufacture, develop, improve, create, raise, or grow property." Crafts businesses come under this rule.

Under the Uniform Capitalization Rule, the cost of a manufacturer's inventory must include the cost of overhead attributable to the manufacturing operation. Such manufacturing overhead becomes part of the cost of the manufactured product, just like the cost of the materials, and cannot be deducted until the product is sold. "Overhead" in this context is very broad and refers to almost everything related to manufacturing: repairs, maintenance, utilities, rent, indirect labor and production supervisory wages, indirect materials, tools and equipment, warehousing costs, administrative costs, insurance, taxes, employee benefits, you name it.

Artists, authors, composers, photographers, and designers who sell original works are exempt from the Uniform Capitalization rules. The exemption applies only to original (one-of-a-kind) work. The exemption does not apply to reproductions, copies, published works, "limited editions," or other production pieces.

Consignment: Consigned inventory is merchandise one business or self-employed individual places with another business for the other business to try to sell. For full information, see **Consignment**.

For more information on inventory and cost-of-goods-sold, see IRS Publication 538, "Accounting Periods and Methods."

Expense category: Cost-of-goods-sold.

Millions of small businesses contribute daily to the economic success of our nation. They pay taxes.

—Robert Dole, former senator

Inventory Tax

Some local and state governments impose an inventory tax (sometimes called a floor tax), a property tax on business inventory. This tax is deductible.
Expense category: Taxes and licenses.

Investment Credit

This is not one, but several tax credits lumped under one heading. Tax credits are different than tax deductions, and can reduce your taxes significantly. Look up individual credits. Also see **Tax Credits**.
Expense category: Tax credits are taken on Form 1040.

Investment Expenses

Money you invest in your own business may or may not be tax deductible, depending on what you spend the money on. Look up the actual expenses. Also see **Start-Up Costs, Organizational Costs**.
Investing (stocks, etc.): Investing (other than investing in your own business) is not considered a business activity by the IRS. Investment expenses, including broker fees, publications, consultants, advice, etc. are not deductible as business expenses.

IRA

Stands for Individual Retirement Arrangement, a tax deferred retirement plan. See **Retirement Plans**.
Expense category: Deducted on the 1040 form.

Janitorial Service

Janitorial and cleaning expenses are part of the **Home Office** deduction. Costs for the entire home are prorated, business versus personal, using the same percentage as the home office. Janitorial and cleaning costs just for the office are fully deductible. If you take the flat rate ("safe harbor") Home Office deduction, these costs are included in the flat rate. See **Home Office**.

Job Credits

For 2013, and possibly for future years if Congress decides to reinstate the credits, "Work Opportunity" tax credits are available for employers who hire certain disadvantaged employees and who hire Native Americans. See **Tax Credits**.

Keogh Plan

A Keogh (also known as an HR-10 plan) is a tax-deferred retirement plan. See **Retirement Plans**.
Expense category: Deducted on the 1040 form.

Kickbacks

Kickbacks often refer to illegal payoffs, bribes, and other wonderful stuff. But sometimes the term kickback refers, rather crudely, to rebates to customers or suppliers, or commissions or rewards paid for referrals. Some states outlaw some kinds of kickbacks. Illegal expenses are not deductible. If a payment is illegal in your state, it is not deductible on your state or federal return. If the kickbacks are legal, they are deductible.
Expense category: Depends on how the money is actually spent.

Land

Land is not deductible until you sell it. Only the cost of a structure can be depreciated.
Real estate developers: Pre-development costs such as planning and design, blueprints, building permits, engineering studies, landscape plans, and the like, cannot be deducted currently, but must be capitalized. Some land developers may be eligible for the **Manufacturer's Deduction**.

Landscaping

According to the IRS, landscaping and lawn care are not deductible for home-based businesses, even if done solely to enhance the image of the business. The only exception to this rule has been for home-based landscapers, if they are using the landscaping to demonstrate or advertise their services.

The Tax Courts have disagreed with the IRS on the landscaping deduction for home businesses and have allowed an allocatable share of landscaping and lawn care costs to be deducted, as part of the Home Office deduction, if the home business had clients visiting on a regular basis and the appearance of the residence and the grounds would be of significance to the business operations. You may want to ask your accountant about this.

If you do decide to deduct landscaping expenses, they will be part of the Home Office deduction, prorated business versus personal. If you take the flat rate ("safe harbor") Home Office deduction, it doesn't matter whether landscaping is deductible or not: all home-related expenses are included in the flat rate. See **Home Office**.

Late Charges

Late charges are deductible, except for government penalties. Penalties for late filing of government forms and tax returns are not deductible.
Expense category: Interest; or Other expenses.

Laundry Services

Laundry services for clothing used exclusively for work are deductible, but only if the clothing is unsuitable for street wear, such as a uniform, costume, or protective gear.
Expense category: Office expense.
Travel: Laundry services for your regular clothing are deductible if you are traveling away from home overnight on business.
Expense category: Travel.

Lawn Care

According to the IRS, landscaping and lawn care are not deductible for home-based businesses, even if done solely to enhance the image of the business. The only exception to this rule has been for home-based landscapers, if they are using the landscaping to demonstrate or advertise their services.

The Tax Courts have disagreed with the IRS on the lawn care deduction for home businesses and have allowed an allocatable share of landscaping and lawn care costs to be deducted, as part of the Home Office deduction, if the home business had clients visiting on a regular basis and the appearance of the residence and the grounds would be of significance to the business operations. You may want to ask your accountant about this.

If you do decide to deduct lawn care expenses, they will be part of the Home Office deduction, prorated business versus personal. If you take the flat rate ("safe harbor") Home Office deduction, it doesn't matter whether lawn care is deductible or not: all home-related expenses are included in the flat rate. See **Home Office**.

Lawyers

See **Attorneys**. Or maybe don't see attorneys.

Leasehold Improvements

Leasehold improvements are building components. The term has nothing to do with leases. See **Building Components.**

Leases

See **Rent**.

Never tell the IRS anything you don't have to.

—Martin S. Kaplan, CPA

Legal Fees

Most legal fees, paralegal fees, filing fees, and related expenses are deductible.

Expense category: Legal and professional services.

Starting or buying a business: Legal fees associated with starting or buying a business cannot be deducted the year paid. They have to be capitalized or amortized over a five-year period. See **Start-Up Costs**, **Buying a Business**.

Licenses

Business licenses and permits, and licenses for any business property are deductible.

Vehicle licenses are deductible if you don't take the standard mileage allowance. See **Vehicles**.

Expense category: Taxes and licenses.

Also see **Licensing Fees** below.

Licensing Fees

Fees paid for the rights to use someone else's work, such as software, or a patent, or an artist's photograph, are deductible, with some restrictions. See the entry for whatever it is you are licensing.

Expense category: Legal and professional services.

Life Insurance (Employers)

Self-employed individuals cannot deduct the cost of life insurance on themselves.

Premiums for group term life insurance paid by an employer on behalf of employees are deductible, but only if the employer is not a beneficiary. If coverage exceeds $50,000, the premiums must be included in the employee's compensation as additional wages, subject to payroll taxes.

Expense category: Insurance.

Limousine Service

Some businesses will have a special occasion to hire a limousine service, which is deductible if appropriate for your business. Be careful if this service is considered an entertainment expense, which is only 50 percent deductible. See **Entertainment**.

Expense category: Other expenses, or possibly Entertainment.

Lists

Fees paid to rent or acquire mailing, email, telephone, or other lists are deductible.

Expense category: Advertising.

Amounts paid to acquire customer accounts usually must be amortized over 15 years.

Expense category: Depreciation. Also fill out Form 4562, "Depreciation and Amortization."

Loan Fees

Loan fees are treated the same as interest. See **Interest Expense**.

Loans

A loan is not income when received and not an expense when paid. Repayment of a loan (principal) is not deductible.

Some loan fees and interest may be deductible. See **Interest Expense**.

Lobbying Expenses

If you spend money to try to influence a federal or state legislator or a federal or state election, you must meet two requirements in order to deduct your expenses: (1) The total amount spent cannot exceed $2,000, and (2) the money must be spent "in house," meaning you cannot hire an outside professional lobbyist.

If part of your dues to a trade or professional association are for political lobbying, that portion of the dues is not deductible.

Lobbying and similar expenses to try to influence local legislation do not come under the above restrictions. You are allowed a deduction for lobbying—and petitioning, and meeting with, and arguing with—your county supervisors, city council members, zoning commissioners, building inspectors, fire marshals, and all those fine local folks who often have a lot of power over local businesses.

Expense category: Legal and professional services.

Political contributions are not deductible.

Lodging

Lodging is deductible while traveling away from home overnight on business.

Corporations can use a per diem rate in lieu of actual costs (noncorporate businesses cannot use the per diem). See **Travel**.

IRS Red Flag Audit Warning: Significant lodging (and related travel) expenses, particularly for small home businesses, are likely to invite an audit. Be sure to document the details of why you were traveling, who you were doing business with, and how the traveling was important to your business.

For more information, see IRS Publication 535, "Business Expenses."

Expense category: Travel.

Employers: Lodging and housing allowances provided by an employer to employees is a tax deductible expense, if the lodging meets the IRS's "ordinary" and "necessary" tests. The lodging is tax-free to the employee if it meets four additional requirements: (1) lodging is for the employer's convenience, (2) is required as a condition of employment, (3) is on the employer's business premises, (4) S corporation employees are eligible but not the S corporation owners themselves. Employees are allowed a deduction for local (in town) lodging if required to participate in a business meeting or other business function by the employer.

For more information, see IRS Publication 15, Circular E, "Employer's Tax Guide."

Expense category: Employee benefit programs.

Logo

The cost of creating a company or product logo is deductible. If the cost is substantial, it may have to be amortized (depreciated) over several years. You should ask your accountant about this.

Expense category: Other expenses; or, if you amortize the cost, Depreciation (also fill out Form 4562, "Depreciation and Amortization").

Graphic designs and package designs are deductible.

Expense category: Advertising.

Long-Term Care Insurance

Long-term care insurance comes under the same eligibility rules as health insurance. See **Health Insurance**.

Long-term care insurance is subject to a dollar limitation, which the IRS changes from year to year, and which varies depending on your age. The age and amount tables can be found in IRS Publication 535, "Business Expenses."

Expense category: Employee benefit programs.

Losses

Casualty and theft losses are deductible, with some limitations. See **Casualty Losses**.

Business losses (showing a loss on your tax return) can be used to offset other income this year, and can also be used to offset profits from other years. See **Net Operating Loss (NOL)**.

Lost income: If a customer or client does not pay you for your work, there is no tax deduction for lost income. You simply don't report any income on your tax return. You have lost the value of your time and effort, but the value of time and effort is not deductible.

If your loss includes goods and materials, you do get a deduction for the cost of the inventory, not the sales price you charged the customer. The deduction is part of your cost-of-goods-sold calculation (see **Inventory**). There is no separate loss deduction.

Machinery

Machinery can be deducted, with limitations, or depreciated. See **Business Assets, Depreciation**.

Expense category: Depreciation. Also fill out Form 4562, "Depreciation and Amortization."

I have the freedom to vacation when I want, arrange my own work schedule, and work at my own pace. I have all the flexibility in the world.

—Dannica Wood, business owner

Magazines

Books, magazines, newsletters, newspapers, and all other publications that are in any way related to your business are deductible.

Expense category: Office expense.

Mailing Lists

Mailing list rentals and purchases are deductible.

Expense category: Advertising

Mailing Supplies and Expenses

Fully deductible.

Expense category: Advertising.

Maintenance

Maintenance and repairs to equipment are deductible. Also see **Repairs**.

Expense category: Repairs and maintenance.

Home: Maintenance expenses for your home are part of the Home Office deduction. Costs for the entire home are prorated, business versus personal, using the same percentage as the home office. Maintenance just for the office is fully deductible. If you take the flat rate ("safe harbor") Home Office deduction, maintenance expenses are included in the flat rate. See **Home Office**.

Manufacturer's Deduction (Employers)

Manufacturers—and some construction firms, land developers, engineering firms, architecture firms, energy producers, software developers, film and videotape producers, farmers and agricultural firms—are allowed a tax deduction equal to 9 percent of net income from domestic (not overseas) production. The maximum deduction is 50 percent of the firm's W-2 wages attributable to production activities. So this deduction applies only to employers.

The Manufacturer's Deduction (also known as the Domestic Production Deduction) is a complex law. The IRS rules go on for 224 pages! But it is a major tax break, benefiting many businesses that manufacture, build, design, or grow products in the United States. Talk to your accountant. Don't let this deduction get away.

Expense category: For businesses other than C corporations, this deduction is taken on the 1040 tax return, not on Schedule C or on the business tax return. This deduction does not reduce your business profit for computing self-employment tax. For C corporations, the deduction is taken on Form 1120.

Manufacturing Supplies

Manufacturing supplies are deductible, but manufacturing supplies that go into the product being manufactured are part of your inventory and cannot be deducted until sold. See **Inventory**.

Expense category: Supplies; or Cost-of-goods-sold.

Marketing

Marketing is a broad term that includes advertising, promotion, entertainment, news releases, catalogs, you name it. Except for entertainment (which is 50 percent deductible), most marketing expenses are fully deductible. Look up each item that comprises your marketing expenses to see what is and is not deductible.

Market Research

Market research expenditures may be deductible currently, or they may have to be capitalized and deducted over a period of years, depending on their nature and the cost.

Market research for a business you haven't yet started may or may not be deductible. See **Start-Up Costs**.

Market research is not eligible for the Research Tax Credit.

Expense category: Varies depending on actual expenses.

Materials and Supplies

Some materials and supplies are deductible, but some must be included in inventory. See **Manufacturing Supplies, Office Supplies, Shipping Supplies**.

Meals

Regular meals at work (for yourself) are generally not deductible.

Meals with a current or prospective customer are 50 percent deductible but only if business is specifically discussed at the meal and if the cost is not "lavish or extravagant." You must have a receipt and write on it who you took out and why. Tips are considered part of the meal and are also 50 percent deductible. Travel to and from the restaurant, including parking, is 100 percent deductible.

Expense category: Meals and entertainment. Travel.

Meals while traveling away from home on business are 50 percent deductible.

Expense category: Meals and entertainment.

Meals that are included as part of a business meeting, sales presentation, or seminar and not billed separately, are probably fully deductible. The IRS has not clearly ruled on this issue, so check with your accountant.

Expense category: Other expenses.

Food samples available to the public are fully deductible. Food and beverages served at business-related events, such as a demonstration or exhibit, are deductible.

Expense category: Advertising.

Interstate truck drivers whose work hours are regulated by the U.S. Department of Transportation can deduct 80 percent of the cost of meals (instead of 50 percent) while on the road.

Expense category: Meals and entertainment.

Businesses selling meals (including caterers): The cost of meals sold to your customers as part of your regular business are 100 percent deductible. Meals that you provide as part of a business meeting or seminar are fully deductible. The food itself is considered inventory. See **Inventory**.

Child care and day care businesses can deduct the full cost of meals provided or can take a special Standard Meal Allowance.

Expense category: There is a category called "Meals and entertainment" but some accountants suggest that child care businesses use "Other expenses" or "Supplies" instead, so as not to wave a red flag at the IRS, which views meals, particularly a big dollar deduction, as a possible audit item.

Employers: Meals provided by an employer to employees are not deductible unless the meals are on the business premises, and are for "the convenience of the employer." There must be a substantial business reason for providing the meals, such as requiring the employees to be on call. If these requirements are met, the cost of employee meals is 100 percent deductible. Employers can deduct the cost of a company cafeteria if more than 50 percent of the meals eaten there were for the employer's convenience.

Occasional meals provided to employees, such as a pizza party, the annual company picnic, or Thanksgiving turkeys you give your employees, are fully (100 percent) deductible. Taking employees out to lunch on a regular basis (not just occasionally or for special occasions) is deductible for the employer but taxable to the employees as wages.

Hotels and resorts that provide meals to employees on the business premises and on company time, may be entitled to a deduction for the cost of the meals. Ask your accountant about this.

If you are an owner-employee of your own S corporation, you are not considered an employee for these employee rules; you yourself are not eligible for the employee deductions.

Expense category: Employee benefit programs.

Also see **Per Diem** and **Standard Meal Allowance.**

Medical Expenses

For the purpose of this deduction, the term "medical expenses" refers to actual medical costs paid to doctors, hospitals, dentists, eye doctors, pharmacies, etc. but not medical insurance. Medical insurance comes under a different set of rules. See **Health Insurance**.

Employers are allowed a full deduction for employees' medical expenses, and for medical expenses of employees' spouses and dependents. This also includes plans known as Health Reimbursement Arrangements (HRAs).

Expense category: Employee benefit programs.

All businesses other than regular C corporations: You, the owner of the business, cannot take a deduction for your own medical expenses (again, we are not talking about medical insurance) unless you are an employee of your own regular C corporation. One exception to this rule is a medical expense (or a drug test) required by law for work, which most accountants say is fully deductible.

Spouse on the payroll: If you hire your spouse as an employee, you possibly may be able to deduct your medical expenses on your business tax return. If your spouse is an employee of your business, on the payroll with regular employee payroll deductions, your spouse *and* family (i.e., you and your children) are eligible for full employee health benefits, and the cost is fully deductible as a business expense. You come under the "Employer" rules above. This is a little-known loophole in the tax law that may be worth a lot of tax savings. But the IRS has sometimes challenged it, often on the grounds that the cost is "unreasonable compensation," that is, more money than is reasonable for the amount and type of work your spouse is doing. I suggest you talk to your accountant.

C Corporations: If you or your spouse is an employee of your own C corporation (not S corporation), your and your family's medical expenses can be deducted as a corporation business expense, but only if you offer the same medical coverage to all of your employees.

Expense category: Employee benefit programs.

Medical Insurance

See **Health Insurance**.

Medicare Tax

Medicare and Social Security are the two combined payroll taxes deducted from every employee's paycheck and collected from every employer. This tax is also called FICA (which stands for Federal Insurance Contributions Act) or just Social Security. Employer's portion is deductible. See **Social Security Tax**.

Expense category: Taxes and licenses.

Medicare tax for self-employed individuals is part of the self-employment tax and is not a deductible business expense. See **Self-Employment Tax**.

Medicare premiums for business owners (that is, the insurance premiums you pay when you are on Medicare) are deductible under the same rules as health insurance. Medicare premiums for spouses may or may not be deductible. The IRS has issued contradictory rulings on this issue. I suggest you check with an accountant.

Meetings

Business meetings are deductible, although you are allowed only a 50 percent deduction for meals. Meetings outside the U.S. are restricted. See: **Travel, Meals, Lodging**.

Expense category: Other expenses.

Membership Fees

Membership fees for business groups, professional organizations, merchant and trade associations, chambers of commerce, etc. are deductible. Membership fees to community service organizations, such as Rotary, Lions, etc., are deductible.

Expense category: Other expenses.

Club memberships: Membership fees in clubs run for pleasure, recreation, or other social purposes are not deductible. These include athletic, luncheon, hotel, airline, sporting and other entertainment or recreational organizations, associations, clubs, and facilities. Even if you use a club membership solely to generate or discuss business, the membership fees are not deductible.

Merchandise

Merchandise is another word for inventory, goods for sale. Generally, it cannot be deducted until sold. See **Inventory**.
Expense category: Cost-of-goods-sold.

The only thing that hurts more than having to pay income tax is not having to pay income tax.

—Sir Thomas R. Dewar, founder, Dewar's Scottish Whiskey

Merchant Associations

Dues and meetings are deductible.
Expense category: Other expenses.
If part of your merchant association dues are for political lobbying, that portion of the dues is not deductible.

Messenger Service

Messenger services are deductible. (This item is dedicated to the memory of John Cipollina.)
Expense category: Office expense.

Mileage Allowance

The IRS has a standard mileage allowance deduction for every business mile driven. This allowance is in lieu of actual vehicle expenses such as gas, oil changes, maintenance, and the cost of the vehicle. See **Vehicles, Standard Mileage Allowance**.

Expense category: Car and truck expenses.

Miscellaneous

Although there are probably a hundred or more miscellaneous expenses a business can legitimately deduct, it is not a good idea to label anything "miscellaneous" on your tax return. The word miscellaneous is vague and can easily invite all kinds of questions from a suspicious auditor, especially if the dollar amounts are significant. It is better to use several smaller, more specific categories, and individually list them on your tax return under "Other Expenses."

Mobile Home

If you are living in a mobile home, the office space can be deducted if it meets the home office requirements. If the mobile home is parked on your home property, being used for business, it is also eligible for the home office deduction. See **Home Office**.

Mobile Phones

Mobile phones come under the same rules as cell phones. If used 100 percent for business, the phones are 100 percent deductible. If used partly for business, you can deduct the percentage of the cost used for business.

Expense category: Office expenses.

Mortgages

A mortgage payment usually includes principal, interest, taxes, and sometimes insurance, all of which come under the Home Office rules. See **Home Office**.

Motorcycles

Motorcycles used for business can be deducted or depreciated like other vehicles. Vehicles have special limitations. See **Vehicles**.

Expense category: The category "Car and truck expenses" is for all vehicle expenses except the cost of the vehicle itself, which is deducted or depreciated under "Depreciation."

Moving Expenses

The business portion of a move is considered a home office expense. See **Home Office**.

Musical Instruments and Equipment

If you are in business as a musician, band, or songwriter, the cost of your instruments and equipment can be deducted or depreciated. See **Business Assets**.

Expense category: Depreciation. Also fill out form 4562, "Depreciation and Amortization."

If you buy a musical instrument to keep in your office just to use for your own enjoyment and relaxation, as many business owners do, is it deductible? I guess you could call it a business expense since it helps you get through the business day. Me, I'd take the deduction. . .

Music System

The office music system can be deducted or depreciated, as long as it is not, to quote the IRS, "lavish or extravagant under the circumstances." See **Business Assets, Depreciation**.

Expense category: Depreciation. Also fill out Form 4562, "Depreciation and Amortization."

The cost of CDs, DVDs, and music downloads are deductible.

Expense category: Office expense.

Multi-Level (Direct Sales) Marketing

See **Buying a Business**.

Net Operating Loss (NOL)

If your business suffers a loss this year, you will owe no income taxes on the business, which I'm sure you know. You may not know that this loss will also offset other income, such as a salary from an outside job or your spouse's wages, and reduce this year's income tax.

You can also use this year's loss to offset income, and reduce taxes, from other years. You are allowed to carry back what the IRS calls a Net Operating Loss (NOL) to apply against prior income and receive a refund of prior years' taxes, even if you were not in business then. The loss can be carried back two years. And if your taxable income for the two prior years is not sufficient to absorb the entire loss, you may carry the balance forward to apply to as many as 20 future years. At your option, you can forgo the two-year carry-back period and apply your NOL entirely to the 20 future years.

A Net Operating Loss, like any other tax deduction, is worth more in a high income year. If the two preceding years generated little or no income tax, you probably will do better to forgo the carry-back, and apply the entire NOL to future years. Also, that way you avoid filing an amended return, which starts the IRS audit statute of limitations running again.

Net Operating Loss is not simply the business loss shown on your tax return. It is a complicated combination of business and non-business income and deductions. I don't include the NOL calculations because they are quite complex, and there's no way to simplify the procedure. Step-by-step instructions are explained in IRS Publication #536, "Net Operating Losses." Don't be put off by their complexity; the NOL deduction may save you a bundle in income taxes.

Expense category: For carrybacks, use Form 1045, "Application for Tentative Refund." For carryforward, individuals use "Other income" line on Form 1040; corporations use "Net operating loss deduction" line on Form 1120.

Network Marketing

See **Buying a Business**.

Newsletters/Newspapers

Books, magazines, newsletters, newspapers, and all other publications are deductible.
Expense category: Office expense.

NOL

"NOL" stands for Net Operating Loss. See **Net Operating Loss**.

Notary Fees

Deductible.
Expense category: Legal and professional services.

Notes

Promissory notes and notes payable are not deductible. The interest is deductible.
Expense category: Interest.

OASDI (Employers)

OASDI stands for Old Age, Survivors, and Disability Insurance. OASDI is another name for the combined Medicare and Social Security payroll taxes deducted from every employee's paycheck and collected from every employer. Employer's portion of OASDI is deductible. See **Social Security Tax**.
Expense category: Taxes and licenses.

Occupational

Occupational licenses, fees, registrations, etc. are deductible.
Expense category: Taxes and licenses.
Occupational training is deductible, within certain restrictions. See **Education Expenses**.

Office

See **Home Office**.
Office outside the home: You can deduct the cost of a separate office outside the home. An outside office does not have to meet the Home Office requirements. However, to get the Home Office deduction for the office in your home—in addition to the deduction for an outside office—the home office must meet the Home Office requirements. A small business with two offices will most likely be challenged in an audit, with the possibility that the IRS will disallow your Home Office deduction, though that shouldn't deter you from taking the Home Office deduction if you meet the IRS requirements. Still, if you are unsure of your standing, or unsure you want to risk an audit, I suggest talking to an accountant.
Expense category: Rent.

Office Equipment

Office equipment can, at your option, be deducted the year of purchase, up to a dollar maximum, or depreciated. See **Business Assets, Depreciation**. Office equipment is deducted in addition to the Home Office deduction. You can deduct office equipment regardless of whether you are eligible for the Home Office deduction or not.
Expense category: Office expense (minor purchases); or Depreciation (also fill out Form 4562, "Depreciation and Amortization").
Here is a partial list of common office equipment:

Adding machines	Humidifiers
Answering machines	Lamps
Brooms	Microwave
Cabinets	Mirrors
Calculators	Music systems
Carts	Phones
Cash registers	Portable heaters
Chairs	Postage meters
Chair mats	Printers
Clocks	Racks
Coat racks	Refrigerators
Coffee makers	Rugs
Computers	Scales
Copiers	Shelves
Credit card terminals	Tables
Decorations (but see **Art Treasures**)	Typewriters (what are those?)
Desks	Vacuum cleaners
Fans	Waste baskets
Fax Machines	Water dispensers
File cabinets	Window shades & blinds

Office Expenses

Most office expenses are deductible. See listings for individual items. Also see **Office Equipment** above and **Office Supplies** below.

Office expenses that are part of the home office itself (building, remodeling, painting, utilities, etc.) are part of the Home Office deduction. See **Home Office**.

Office in the Home

See **Home Office**.

Office Supplies

"Office supplies" is a catch-all term. I tend to lump all kinds of low-cost business purchases in this category. It is a reasonably accurate description, and sure sounds better and less dubious than "Miscellaneous" or "Other Expenses." Office supplies are deductible.

Expense category: Office supplies.
Office supplies include:

Account books	Kleenex
Bank checks	Knives
Batteries	Labels
Beverages	Ledger paper
Blades	Ledgers
Books	Letter openers
Bottled water	Light bulbs
Boxes	Magazines
Brooms	Maps
Business cards	Moisteners
Carpal tunnel wrist supports	Mops
Calendars	Newsletters
Cartons	Organizers
CDs and DVDs	Paper
Cleaning supplies	Paper clips
Clipboards	Pencils
Coffee	Pens
Coffee	Periodicals
Coffee	Plants
Computer disks	Plant hangers
Directories	Postage stamps
Dust covers	Post-Its
Dust pans	Printer ribbons
Envelopes	Rolodex
Erasers	Rubber bands
Fasteners	Rubber stamps
File holders	Rulers
Fire extinguisher	Safety glasses
First aid kit	Scissors
Flashlight	Signs
Folders	Small tools
Forms	Soap
Glue	Software (inexpensive)
Goldfish bowls	Stamp pads
Greeting cards	Staple removers
Hole punchers	Staplers
Invoices	Stationery

Tape

Tape dispensers

Toner

Towels

Videos

Wall and office decorations

White-out

And most important, Emergency

    Rations:

    Emergency box of chocolates

    Emergency bag of peanuts

    Emergency bottle of brandy

Offshoring

See **Foreign Expenses**.

"Off the Books" Payments

"Books" is another term for ledgers, your record of business income and expenditures. "Off the books" refers to a payment, in cash, that you intentionally chose not to record in your ledgers. And now you want to find out if it is deductible? Was the payment legal? If it was legal, it probably is deductible. If it was illegal it is not deductible. For more great information about off-the-books payments, see **Under the Table**, which means the same thing.

Expense category: Varies depending on actual expenses.

Operating Expenses

"Operating expenses" is a general term for the day-to-day costs of running a business. The IRS does not define operating expenses and does not have a category called operating expenses. Look up the individual expenses to see what is and isn't deductible.

Operating Losses

Business losses (showing a loss on your tax return) can be used to offset other income this year, and can also be used to offset profits from other years. See **Net Operating Loss**.

Expense category: For carrybacks, use Form 1045, "Application for Tentative Refund." For carryforward, individuals use "Other income" line on Form 1040, corporations use "Net operating loss deduction" line on Form 1120.

This agency intends to become an efficient consumer service organization, keeping taxpayers satisfied.

—IRS press release

Organizational Costs

Business expenses incurred before you start operating your business come under a different tax rule than expenses incurred once you are officially open for business.

The IRS has two categories of costs associated with starting a business: Start-Up Costs, and Organizational Costs. Start-Up Costs apply to all businesses, and are deductible, with limitations, in addition to Organizational Costs. See **Start-Up Costs**.

Organizational Costs apply only to businesses being set up as corporations. Organizational Costs are the legal and accounting services, and government filing fees to set up the business (though not the cost of selling stock). No more than $5,000 of Organizational Costs can be deducted the first year of business. Expenses in excess of the $5,000 maximum must be amortized over 15 years. The $5,000 deduction phases out, dollar for dollar, if organizational costs exceed $50,000.

The first-year deduction is optional. You can deduct less than the maximum this year, and spread the balance over 15 years. If your new business hasn't earned much money, and will owe little or no taxes for the current year, by spreading out the organizational costs over 15 years, you will save on future years' taxes.

Organizations

Dues and other expenses for business groups, professional organizations, merchant and trade associations, chambers of commerce, etc. are deductible. Dues to community service organizations, such as Rotary, Lions, etc., are deductible.

Dues and membership fees in organizations run for pleasure, recreation, or other social purposes are not deductible. These include athletic, luncheon, hotel, airline, sporting, and other entertainment or recreational organizations, associations, clubs, and facilities. Even if you use your membership solely to generate or discuss business, the dues are not deductible. Sometimes the term "business club" is used to describe such a facility. If the "business" club is not a business organization, the dues are not deductible.

If part of your dues to a trade or professional association or other organization is for political lobbying, that portion of the dues is not deductible.

The cost of attending meetings and seminars is deductible, although you are allowed only a 50 percent deduction for meals.

See **Travel, Meals, Lodging**.

Expense category: Other expenses.

Other Expenses

I list this because there is a category on the tax return called "Other Expenses." But you should not label any expenses "Other Expenses." Like the category Miscellaneous, "other" is too vague, and can easily invite questions from a suspicious IRS auditor, especially if the dollar amounts are significant. It is okay to list expenses under "Other Expenses" on your tax return, but spell out what the expenses are actually for.

Expense category: Other expenses.

Outside Contractors

"Outside" refers not to the great outdoors, but to outside the business, not an employee. The terms outside contractor and independent contractor are used interchangeably. The term "free agent" means the same thing. Fees paid to outside contractors are deductible. See **Independent Contractors**.

Expense category: Commissions and fees.

Outstanding Checks

Outstanding checks are checks you have written that have not been deposited or cashed yet. Sooner or later, the checks almost always get deposited or cashed. Give them a little more time to see if they'll clear on your next your bank statement. If they don't, see **Uncashed Checks**.

Overhead

Overhead is a broad term and usually refers to your fixed costs, the dozens of large and small expenses you pay whether you are generating income or not: rent, utilities, phone, insurance, office supplies, permits and licenses, payroll, and the cost and maintenance of furniture, tools, and equipment. These costs cannot be tied directly to a product or service.

Most overhead is deductible, but not as a lump sum. Look up each item that comprises your overhead to see what is and isn't deductible.

Manufacturers: Manufacturing overhead is not deductible immediately. It is added to the cost of your inventory. See **Inventory**.

Owner's Draw

The owner of an unincorporated business (sole proprietorship, partnership, or limited liability company) cannot get a tax-deductible salary or wage. Payments to owners are known as "draw." See **Draw, Paying Yourself**.

Package Design Costs

See **Design Costs**.

Packaging Materials

Cartons, boxes, bottles, and other containers and packaging materials that are used to hold the goods you sell, are considered inventory.

See **Inventory**. If, however, the cost of the containers or packaging is not significant or they are used only occasionally, most businesses write them off currently as shipping supplies.
Expense category: Supplies.

Painting

Home office: Painting costs are part of the Home Office deduction. If you take the flat rate ("safe harbor") Home Office deduction, painting costs are included in the flat rate. See **Home Office**.

Inventory: Painting inventory (including manufactured and crafted goods) is included as part of the cost of the goods. See **Inventory**.

Other: Most other business painting costs can be deducted currently, though a major paint job on equipment may have to be depreciated. *Expense category:* Repairs and maintenance.

Paralegal Fees

Paralegal fees are deductible. But see **Start-Up Costs**.
Expense category: Legal and professional fees.

Parents on Payroll

Children who hire their parents get no special tax breaks. The parents are considered regular employees, subject to all regular employment and income taxes, except Federal Unemployment Tax (FUTA). Parents are exempt from FUTA tax.
Expense category: Wages.

Parking

Parking at your regular place of work is not deductible. The IRS considers this a commuting expense. All other business parking costs are deductible. If you take the standard mileage allowance, parking (other than parking at your regular place of work) is deductible in addition to the mileage allowance. Parking tickets are not deductible (towing charges are).

Expense category: Car and truck expenses.

Employers: If you provide parking to employees on or near your business, the costs are deductible. You can reimburse employees up to $250 per month, and the parking is tax-free to the employee. This deduction applies to employees, not to self-employed individuals and not to owners of S corporations, who must follow the parking law explained above.

Expense category: Employee benefit programs.

Parking Tickets

Not deductible. Fines for breaking the law are not deductible.

Parties

A company or holiday party where all employees are invited is 100 percent deductible. They don't have to all show up, but they all have to be invited to get the deduction.

A sales meeting, show, or exhibit that includes refreshments, if it is primarily a business event where business is conducted, is 100 percent deductible.

Business parties, luncheons, dinners, or events that are primarily parties, even though thrown to promote your business, come under entertainment and are 50 percent deductible. See **Entertainment**.

Expense category: Office expense; Advertising; or Entertainment.

Parts

Parts that a repair shop sells or uses, parts that you use or sell in a trade such as a plumber or electrician, and parts that go into a manufactured product are inventory, and cannot be deducted until sold. See **Inventory**. If the parts are just supplies or do not have significant value, most businesses write them off when purchased.

Expense category: Cost-of-goods-sold, if inventory. Supplies, if they are a minor expense.

Supplies that a repair shop sells or uses, and supplies that you use or sell in your trade, such as a plumber or electrician, can be written off when purchased. But if the supplies are replacement parts with significant value, they are considered part of inventory, and cannot be deducted until sold. See **Inventory**.

Manufacturers who keep a "pool" of rotating spare parts to replace defective parts, can sometimes depreciate those parts instead of including them in inventory. Check with your accountant.

Expense category: Depreciation. Also fill out Form 4562, "Depreciation and Amortization."

Parts that go into machinery or equipment that your business owns and uses (not for sale) can be deducted. If the parts are expensive and used for a major repair job, however, the parts may have to be depreciated. See **Repairs, Business Assets, Depreciation**.

Expense category: Repairs and maintenance; or Depreciation (also fill out Form 4562, "Depreciation and Amortization").

Place for most people is important. Space is a way that people can divide their lives so they have a life outside of their work. If you want your home office to be truly heavenly, make sure you can walk away from it.

—Sarah Edwards, home business consultant

Patents

Patent fees are amortized (depreciated) over their useful life, which can be as long as twenty years.

Some of the costs of researching and designing whatever is being patented may have to be deducted over several years, and some of the costs can be deducted currently. Check with your accountant.

Expense category: Depreciation. Also fill out Form 4562, "Depreciation and Amortization."

Paying Yourself

If your business is a sole proprietorship, partnership, or limited liability company, you the owner (or co-owner) are not an employee of your business. You cannot hire yourself as an employee. This is a point of law often misunderstood by new business people. You cannot pay yourself a wage and deduct it as a business expense.

You may withdraw (that is, pay yourself) as much or as little money as you want, but this "draw" is not a wage, you do not pay payroll taxes on it, and you cannot claim a business deduction for it. The profit of your business, which is computed without regard to your draws, is your "wage" and is included on your personal income tax return.

Corporations: If your business is a corporation, you are an employee of your business. Your salary is a deductible expense of your business. See **Payroll**.

If your corporation is not making any money or losing money, you may not want to pay yourself a salary until the corporation is making a taxable profit. Otherwise you'll be paying payroll taxes and personal income taxes on the salary but getting no tax breaks for your corporation. This is an area you should discuss with an accountant.

Expense category: Wages.

Payroll (Employers)

Employee wages are deductible. Payroll taxes that you, the employer, pay on behalf of your employees, such as Social Security, Medicare, and other federal or state requirements, are deductible.

Corporations: If your business is a corporation, you are an employee of your business, and your salary (and employer's portion of payroll taxes) are a deductible expense of your business.

Disadvantaged employees: A Work Opportunity tax credit was available for hiring certain disadvantaged employees in 2013 and may be extended to 2014. See **Tax Credits**.

For more information, see IRS Publication 15, "Circular E, Employer's Tax Guide." Also see **Reimbursements, Fringe Benefits**.

Expense category: Wages.

Paying yourself: If your business is a sole proprietorship, partnership, or limited liability company (LLC), you the owner are not an employee of your business. You cannot hire yourself as an employee. See **Paying Yourself**.

Payroll Services (Employers)

Payroll services are deductible.
Expense category: Legal and professional services.

Payroll Taxes (Employers)

Payroll taxes that you the employer pay on behalf of your employees, such as Social Security, Medicare, and other federal or state requirements (the employer's portion of the taxes), are fully deductible.

Payroll taxes you withhold from employees' wages (the employee's portion of the taxes) are not deductible. You are entitled to a deduction for the full wages you pay, before deducting the taxes.

Payroll taxes that you pay on your own wages are deductible only if your business is a corporation (and then, again, only the employer's portion of the payroll taxes).

If your business is a sole proprietorship, partnership or limited liability company, you the owner (or co-owner) cannot deduct your own payroll (self-employment) taxes. However, you are allowed a tax deduction on your personal 1040 return for part of the self-employment tax you pay. See **Self-Employment Tax**.

Expense category: Taxes and licenses.

Penalties

Tax penalties and fines for violation of the law are not deductible.

Penalties for not meeting contract requirements, and any other fines or penalties that do not involve breaking the law, are deductible.

Expense category: Other expenses.

Pension Plans

See **Retirement Plans**.

Per Diem

"Per diem" is French, or maybe Latin, for "by the day," a daily allowance. The IRS has established per-diem lodging and food deductions for people traveling away from home overnight on business. Food and lodging per diems apply to corporations and to employees only. Self-employed individuals can use the food, but not the lodging per diems.

Per-diem rates for meals are only 50 percent deductible, because meals are only 50 percent deductible. Per-diem rates for lodging are 100 percent deductible.

Here's the best part: At your option, you can take either the per diem (if you are eligible) or the actual costs. If the per diem is higher, deduct the per diem. If actual costs are higher, deduct the costs. To use another French (or maybe Latin) expression, *c'est la vie*.

For per-diem rates and details, see IRS Publication #1542, "Per Diem Rates." Also see **Travel, Standard Meal Allowance**.

Expense category: Travel.

Periodicals

Business periodicals, magazines, newsletters, newspapers, etc. are deductible.

Expense category: Office expense.

Permits

Business permits and licenses are deductible. Permits obtained before starting your business may have to be included in start-up costs. See **Start-Up Costs**.

Expense category: Taxes and licenses.

Building permits are part of the costs related to the home office. See **Home Office**.

Personal Property

In tax law, personal property refers to tangible business assets other than real estate. Business machinery, equipment, tools, furniture, etc. are personal property. In this context, the word "personal" does not refer to non-business.

Personal property can be deducted the year acquired or depreciated over several years, depending on several factors. See **Business Assets, Depreciation**.

Expense category: Depreciation. Also fill out Form 4562, "Depreciation and Amortization."

Personal Property Tax

Some states and localities have a property tax on business assets such as machinery and furniture, similar to the property tax on real estate. This is known as a personal property tax (see **Personal Property** above). Although the tax uses the word "personal," this is not a tax on non-business property. This is a business tax, and it is fully deductible.

Personal property taxes can be quite high if your assets are assessed at a high value. You should examine the personal property tax bill, and make sure retired or sold assets are not included, and that older assets are not overvalued.

Expense category: Taxes and licenses.

Petty Cash

Petty cash is a small fund of cash some businesses keep on hand to pay small expenses. The expenses are usually for office supplies and are deductible. See **Office Supplies**.

Expense category: Office expense.

Photocopies

Deductible.
Expense category: Office expense.

Plants

Office plants (the growing kind, not boilers and electricity-generating plants) and their upkeep are fully deductible.
Expense category: Office expense.
Nurseries: Plants are considered inventory. See **Inventory**. Some plant production costs, however, are currently deductible. You should consult an accountant familiar with the nursery business, as there are special IRS rules for nursery businesses.

Not taking a legitimate tax deduction is like walking into a store and paying more for the merchandise than the store wants.

—Sam Leandro, business owner, Willits, CA

Points

Points and other loan origination fees are considered interest. See **Interest**.

Political Contributions

Political campaign contributions, to a candidate or to a political party, are not deductible. Advertising in a political program or buying tickets to a political event are not deductible. So how do all these huge corporations funnel hundreds of thousands of dollars into political campaigns to try to buy elections?

Lobbying expenses are sometimes deductible. See **Lobbying Expenses**.

Postage

Postage, post office box rents, and postal permits are deductible.
Expense category: Office expense.

Post Office Box

Post office box rents and mailbox store rents ("suites" as the mail order connoisseurs call them), are deductible.
Expense category: Office expense.

Prepayments

Prepaid expenses that do not extend beyond twelve months (with some important exceptions, below) can be deducted when paid, even though the expenses are partly for the next year. For example, you could pay for a maintenance contract that ran from December of this year to December of next year, and deduct the entire amount this year.

The exceptions: The IRS says that prepaid interest, rent, leases, and prepaid taxes are not deductible until the year they apply to, even for cash basis taxpayers. Some tax courts disagree, and have applied the 12-month rule to these expenses. You should check with your accountant.

Also, prepayments in the current year that apply entirely to the next year, even if they meet the 12-month rule, in some cases may not be deductible until next year. Again, you should check with your accountant.

Prepaid expenses that cover more than twelve months cannot be deducted until the year the expenses apply to. Only the current year's portion can be written off this year.
Expense category: Varies depending on actual expenses.

Presentations

Business presentations are deductible, although you are allowed only a 50 percent deduction for meals. Also see: **Travel, Meals, Lodging**.
Expense category: Other expenses.

Prizes

Prizes to customers and suppliers are deductible, within limits. See **Awards**.

Expense category: Advertising; or Other expenses.

For prizes given to employees, see **Awards**.

Product Development

Product development expenses are usually deductible, and may also be eligible for a Research and Experimentation Tax Credit. See **Tax Credits**.

Some development expenses that will benefit future years may have to be capitalized, and deducted over a period of at least five years. You should discuss these expenses with your accountant.

Expense category: Other expenses.

Professional Associations and Organizations

Dues and meetings are deductible.

Expense category: Other expenses.

If part of your dues to a trade or professional association are for political lobbying, that portion of the dues is not deductible.

Professional Services

Professional, legal, and accounting services are deductible. But see **Start-Up Costs**.

Expense category: Legal and professional services.

Profit Sharing Plans (Employers)

Corporate profit sharing plans are deductible.

There is also something called a profit sharing plan that is really a Keogh (HR-10) retirement plan. See **Retirement Plans**.

Expense category: Pension and profit sharing plans.

Promissory Notes

A promissory note is a promise to pay money you owe, basically a loan agreement. The promissory note itself is not deductible, but the interest is.

Expense category: Interest (for the interest only).

Promotion

Promotional expenses are deductible. These may include free handouts, samples, news releases, audio and video productions, brochures, premiums, small gifts, greeting cards, or some service, performance, or show.

Sometimes there may be a fine line between what is "promotion" and what is "entertainment." Promotion expenses are fully deductible, and entertainment is limited to a 50 percent deduction. The wise taxpayer carefully defines the expenses.

Expense category: Advertising; or Other expenses.

Property Taxes

Property taxes for your home are part of the **Home Office** deduction. Property taxes are prorated, business versus personal, using the same percentage as the home office. If you take the flat rate ("safe harbor") Home Office deduction, property taxes are included in the flat rate. See **Home Office**. Home property taxes can also be deducted on Schedule A of your personal 1040 return if you itemize expenses.

Real estate developers: If you purchase land that you plan to build on and sell, the property taxes are not currently deductible. The taxes are capitalized.

Protective Gear

Cost of gear is deductible. Cost of cleaning is deductible.

Expense category: Supplies.

Publications

Books, magazines, newsletters, newspapers, and all other business-related publications are deductible.

Expense category: Office expense.

Punitive Damages

Punitive damages imposed by a government agency for breaking the law are not deductible. Any other punitive damages (such as for breach of contract), late charges, and the like, are deductible.

Expense category: Other expenses.

Raw Materials

"Raw materials" is a manufacturing term for the parts that go into whatever is being manufactured. Raw materials are inventory, and cannot be deducted until sold. See **Inventory**.

Expense category: Cost-of-goods-sold.

Real Estate

Real estate is buildings and land. See **Home Office**.

Buildings (other than the home office) can be depreciated, or in some cases written off the year of purchase. Land cannot be written off until sold. See **Buildings, Depreciation, Land**.

Expense category: Depreciation (for buildings). Also fill out Form 4562, "Depreciation and Amortization."

Real Estate Taxes

See **Property Taxes**.

Rebates

Rebates paid out, if legal, are deductible. Many states outlaw kick-backs and bribes, however, and some types of rebates may fall into this legal swamp. If rebates are outlawed in your state, they are not deductible on your federal return, even if there is no federal law outlawing the expenditure. State law controls the deductibility.

Rebates received are not income; they are price reductions and reduce the cost (and reduce the deduction) for what you purchased.

Also, see **Refunds**.

Expense category: Depends on how the money is actually spent.

Record Keeping

Record keeping, accounting, bookkeeping, and similar services are deductible. Record keeping software and Internet record keeping services are deductible.

Cost of preparing business tax returns is fully deductible. For sole proprietors, only the cost of preparing the business part of your 1040 tax return (schedule C and related schedules) is deductible as a business expense.

Expense category: Legal and professional services.

Recreational Vehicles (RVs)

RVs used for business can be deducted or depreciated like other vehicles. See **Vehicles**. Keep in mind that all business deductions must meet the IRS's "ordinary" and "necessary" tests explained at the beginning of this book.

Expense category: The category "Car and truck expenses" is for all vehicle expenses except the cost of the vehicle itself, which is deducted or depreciated under "Depreciation." You also file Form 4562, "Depreciation and Amortization."

RV as a home office: If you are living in an RV, the office space can be deducted if it meets the home office requirements. If the RV is parked on your home property, being used for business, it is also eligible for the home office deduction. See **Home Office**.

Referrals

Commissions or fees paid for referrals are deductible.
Expense category: Commissions and fees.

Commissions paid to acquire new customers who sign long term contracts, may have to be capitalized, and deducted over a period of years. The IRS says the deduction must be spread over the average number of years new customers stay with the business. This is something you should ask your accountant about.

Refunds

Money you refund to a customer is deductible. On the tax return, these sales refunds are shown in the income section, as a reduction to income, rather than in the expense section.
Expense category: Returns and allowances.

Rehabilitation of Buildings

Renovations for your home are added to the cost of the building. See **Buildings**.

Renovations for other business buildings have to be added to the cost of the building and depreciated. See **Depreciation**.

Reimbursements

Self-employed individuals who get reimbursed by clients for out-of-pocket expenses usually include the reimbursements as part of total income, and deduct the expenses as regular business expenses.

Employers reimbursing employees: When an employer reimburses an employee for out-of-pocket business expenses, the employer is entitled to a tax deduction for the expenses.

The reimbursement is not part of the employee's wages, not subject to payroll taxes, and not included on the employee's W-2 wage statement—but only if the employer and employee follow some strict IRS rules regarding reimbursements. Employers are required to have a written policy (called "an accountable plan") regarding reimbursements to employees. Employees must give the employer documents to substantiate the expenses.

Employee reimbursement, especially reimbursements that are part of some "salary reduction" program, can be a tricky area of law. The IRS often views reimbursements as wages in disguise, an attempt to avoid payroll taxes. Tool reimbursement plans in particular are a "red flag" to the IRS. Talk to your accountant about this.

If the employer's reimbursement exceeds the employee's actual expenses, the excess is considered additional wages, deductible as payroll, and subject to payroll taxes.

Businesses reimbursing the business owners: If you are a partner in a partnership or an owner of a Limited Liability Company (LLC) your business can reimburse you for your out-of-pocket expenses, and the business gets the deduction. But the IRS requires you to have the same written "accountable plan" discussed above under "Employers Reimbursing Employees."

If you own your own corporation, you are an employee of your business. The above "Employers Reimbursing Employees" applies to you.

If you are a sole proprietor, you are exempt from this reimbursement rule. Any money you spend for your business is a business deduction, whether you spend it from your personal funds or from your business funds. There is no need to reimburse yourself.

Expense category: Depends on how the money is actually spent.

Relocation Costs

See **Moving Expenses.**

It's very hard to tell struggling small businesses why they should be honest and pay their taxes when the big companies are hiring lobbyists to get out of their tax liability.

—Dean Baker, director, Center for Economic Policy and
Research

Remodeling

Remodeling expenses are part of the costs related to the home office. See **Home Office**.

Renovations

Renovations for your home are added to the cost of the building. See **Buildings**.

Also see **Tax Credits** for information about the Rehabilitation Tax Credit and the Disabled Access Credit.

Rent

Home: If you rent or lease your home, the rent expenses are part of the Home Office deduction, prorated business versus personal, using the same percentage as the home office. If you take the flat rate ("safe harbor") Home Office deduction, the expenses are included in the flat rate. See **Home Office**.

Other: Leases and rentals for vehicles, equipment, or additional business spaces (such as a separate warehouse) are deductible (but see *Automobile Leases* below).

Prepayments: The IRS says that prepaid lease payments are not deductible until the year they apply to. Some tax courts disagree. You may want to ask your accountant about this.

Canceling a lease: A payment made to cancel a lease is deductible (other than for the home office, which comes under the Home Office limitations). A payment made to cancel a lease in order to get a more favorable lease, is deducted over the term of the new lease.

Expense category: Rent or lease.

Lease-purchase arrangements are considered purchases, not leases, and handled like any other purchase. A lease where you can purchase the equipment for a nominal fee at the end of the lease period is also considered a purchase.

Expense category: Depreciation.

Automobile leases: Automobile leases, if 30 days or longer, are not 100 percent deductible. The IRS has a table, called "Inclusion

Amounts for Cars," that shows how much of an auto lease can be deducted. See IRS Publication 463 for the table. This rule does not apply to trucks, vans, or heavy sport utility vehicles.

Leasing equipment from employees: Payments to employees for use of their equipment (sometimes referred to as "tool allowances") are considered taxable wages, not lease payments, unless the payments are part of a formal accountable plan. The is a hot-button issue for the IRS. You should talk to an experienced accountant about this.

Repairs

Home: The cost of repairs to the home are part of the Home Office deduction. Costs for the entire home are prorated, business versus personal, using the same percentage as the home office. Repairs just for the office are fully deductible. If you take the flat rate ("safe harbor") Home Office deduction, repair expenses are included in the flat rate. See **Home Office**.

Other repairs: Minor repairs on other business property are fully deductible as a current expense.

Major repairs: Major repairs may have to be treated as a permanent (capital) investment and handled in the same manner as the purchase of a depreciable asset. See **Business Assets, Depreciation**. However, the Tax Courts have been overruling the IRS, allowing the write-off of major repairs. I suggest you talk to your accountant about this expense.

Expense category: Repairs and maintenance; or Depreciation.

Research

Research expenses (Research and Development—R&D; Research and Experimentation—R&E) are usually deductible, and may also be eligible for special tax credits. See **Tax Credits**.

Some research expenses that will benefit future years may have to be capitalized, and deducted over a period of at least five years. You should discuss these expenses with your accountant.

What is a research expense? The term can be defined broadly but usually refers to developing, testing, refining, or improving a product or service. The Tax Court has ruled that software development may be considered a research expense, eligible for the tax credit; the IRS disagrees, so I suggest you check with your accountant.

Expense category: Other expenses.

Reserves

Generally, reserves are funds set aside for some future use or in anticipation of some unplanned expense or loss. Nothing is actually spent, and no tax deduction is allowed.

Reserves for bad debts: Funds set aside in anticipation of bad debts are not deductible. Actual bad debts are deductible. See **Bad Debts**.

Reserves for self-insurance: Funds set aside in anticipation of having a claim that might otherwise be covered by insurance, are not deductible. If you have a loss, you may then have a deduction. See **Casualty Losses**.

Small business is where we have the most trouble.

—Charles O. Rossotti, Former IRS Commissioner

Restoration

Restoration cost for your home must usually be added to the cost of the building. See **Buildings**.

Restoration and reconditioning of other business assets, if the cost is not significant, can be deducted the year incurred. Major restoration expenses may have to be treated as a permanent (capital) investment and handled in the same manner as the purchase of a depreciable asset. See **Business Assets, Depreciation**.

Expense category: Repairs and maintenance; or Depreciation (also fill out Form 4562, "Depreciation and Amortization").

Retirement Plans

You may invest a portion of your profit in a special tax-deferred retirement plan and pay no income taxes on the money invested or the interest earned until you retire and withdraw the funds.

Retirement contributions an employer makes on behalf of employees are deductible as a business expense.

Retirement contributions a business owner makes for himself or herself are not considered business deductions (except for some corporate plans) and do not reduce the taxable profit of the business. The contributions, if they meet IRS requirements, reduce the owner's personal income taxes.

There are several tax-deferred retirement plans available to business owners and their employees. Each plan has different options, different contributions, different deadlines for making contributions, and, most important to employers, different requirements for including your employees in the plans. You can choose just one plan, or you may be able to set up multiple plans. The different retirement plans include:

1. Individual Retirement Arrangement (IRA).
2. Roth IRA, a different kind of IRA (named after Senator Roth, who sponsored the legislation).
3. Self-employed Pension Plan (SEP or SEP-IRA).
4. Keogh Plan, also called HR-10 Plan (named after Congressman Keogh and his bill number).
5. Deferred Compensation Plan, more commonly called a 401(k) Plan (named after the IRS Code section number).
6. Savings Incentive Match Plan for Employees (SIMPLE).
7. Corporate Retirement Plan. Also known as an ERISA Plan (Employee Retirement Income Security Act).

Talk to your accountant about the different plans, and which plan will best suit your own needs, your budget, and your employees. Banks and insurance companies offer all of the retirement plans, and can provide you with full details about each plan.

See IRS Publication 590, "Individual Retirement Arrangements" and Publication 560, "Retirement Plans for the Small Business."

Expense category: Depends on the kind of plan.

The cost of setting up a retirement plan may be eligible for a start-up tax credit. See **Tax Credits.**

Returned Checks

A polite term for bounced (bad) checks. Bounced checks are deductible as a bad debt expense. See **Bounced Checks, Bad Debts.**
Expense category: Bad debts.

Returned Goods

Refunds on returned goods are deducted from your income in figuring your taxes. See **Refunds**.

The goods should be added back into inventory if they are still salable, or left off the inventory if they are unsalable. At the end of the year, the returned goods become part of your inventory and cost-of-goods-sold calculations. See **Inventory.**

Expense category: Returns and allowances.

If you sell goods as returnable, you cannot take a deduction in anticipation of future returns. After the goods are actually returned, you get to reduce your income as explained under **Refunds.**

Rewards

Rewards to customers, vendors, and other non-employees are deductible, within limits. See **Awards**.

Expense category: Advertising, or Other expenses.

Rewards to employees, other than token non-monetary gifts, are usually considered wages, taxable to the employee and subject to regular payroll taxes. However, employees can receive "employee achievement awards" that are not considered taxable wages. See **Awards**.

Roads

Expenses associated with private roads and driveways are part of the Home Office deduction, prorated business versus personal using the same percentage as the home office. If you take the flat rate ("safe harbor") Home Office deduction, the expenses are included in the flat rate. See **Home Office**.

Robbery Losses

Deductible, but with special rules. See **Casualty Losses**.

Royalties

Royalties you pay are deductible.
Expense category: Commissions and fees.

Safe Deposit Box

Safe deposit boxes are deductible.
Expense category: Office expense.

Safety Equipment

Safety equipment, first aid kits, fire extinguishers, and the like are deductible. Large structural safety equipment may have to be added to the cost of the building and depreciated. See **Depreciation**.
Expense category: Supplies; or Depreciation (also fill out Form 4562, "Depreciation and Amortization").

Salaries

Employee salaries are deductible. See **Payroll**.
Expense category: Wages.
Also see **Paying Yourself**.

Sales Refunds

Money you refund to a customer is deductible. On your tax return, these sales refunds are shown in the income section, as a reduction to income, rather than in the expense section.
Expense category: Returns and allowances.

Sales Returns

Refunds on returned goods are deducted from your income in figuring your taxes. See **Sales Refunds** above. There is no additional deduction for returned goods. The goods should be added back into inventory if they are still salable, or left off the inventory if they are unsalable. At the end of the year, the returned goods become part of your inventory and cost-of-goods-sold calculations. See **Inventory.**

Expense category: Returns and allowances.

Sales Tax

Sales tax paid on business equipment, depreciable assets, and vehicles, should be added to the cost of the equipment, and deducted or depreciated. See **Business Assets, Depreciation.** Do not deduct the sales tax separately.

Sales tax paid on supplies and similar purchases should be added to the cost of the goods or services purchased, and deducted. Again, do not deduct the sales tax separately.

Vehicles: If you take the standard mileage allowance, the sales tax on the vehicle is considered part of allowance and cannot be deducted separately. See **Standard Mileage Allowance.**

Sales tax collected from your customers: Most businesses include sales tax in gross income, and deduct it as a business expense. Net effect is zero.

Expense category: Taxes and licenses (for sales tax collected from customers and remitted to the government).

Samples

Samples of your merchandise, given to prospective buyers or to people who might review or publicize your products, are deductible. You deduct the cost of the samples (not the retail or market value) as part of cost-of-goods-sold. See **Inventory.**

Expense category: Cost-of-goods-sold.

Scholarships

Scholarships given to employees are deductible. See **Education Expenses**. Scholarships given to an employee's spouse or children are usually considered taxable wages, but there are some exceptions. You should ask your accountant about this.

Scholarships given to members of the community as a gesture of goodwill may be deductible as a promotional expense. Again, check with your accountant.

SECA Tax

"SECA" stands for Self-employment Contributions Act, and refers to the self-employment tax. See **Self-Employment Tax**. It is not deductible.

Section 179 Deduction

This refers to the tax law that allows a business to fully deduct some assets the year of purchase rather than depreciate them over several years. Also known as the First-Year Write-Off. See **Business Assets**.

Expense category: Depreciation. Also fill out Form 4562, "Depreciation and Amortization."

Security

Security services and security systems are part of the Home Office deduction. Costs for the entire home are prorated, business versus personal, using the same percentage as the home office. Costs just for the office are fully deductible. If you take the flat rate ("safe harbor") Home Office deduction, security expenses are included in the flat rate. See **Home Office**.

These days, a person's office is wherever his computer is, and there are very few limits to what can be done at home. But the essential message you must convey to clients, to suppliers, to bankers, to investors, is that you are every bit as serious, sophisticated, and growth minded as you would be in any other location.

—Bill Tann, Internet consultant, New York City

Self-Employment Tax

Self-employment tax, also known as SECA (Self-employment Contributions Act), is combined Social Security and Medicare tax for self-employed individuals. Sole proprietors, partners in partnerships, and active owners of limited liability companies are subject to self-employment tax. The tax is not imposed on owners (shareholders) of small corporations, who are employees of the business and pay regular employee payroll taxes.

You cannot deduct self-employment tax as a business expense. However, you are allowed a tax deduction on your personal 1040 return.

Expense category: Taken on Form 1040.

Spouses who are both self-employed figure their self-employment taxes separately, each paying the tax on their separate incomes.

Self-Insurance

Self-insurance is not really insurance at all, because no insurance policy is purchased. Not deductible.

Putting money aside in a separate bank account or reserve account (to self-insure for a possible emergency or loss) is not deductible until you actually spend the money.

Seminars

Most business seminars are deductible, but see **Education Expenses**.

Expense category: Other expenses.

SEP/SEP-IRA

SEP stands for Simplified Employee Pension plan, a tax-deferred retirement plan. Also known as SEP-IRA. See **Retirement Plans**.
Expense category: Deducted on Form 1040.

Service Contracts

Service contracts and extended warranties are usually deductible. However, see **Prepayments.**
Expense category: Other expenses.
Service contracts related to the home or the home office are part of the Home Office deduction. Costs for the entire home are prorated, business versus personal, using the same percentage as the home office. Costs just for the office are fully deductible. If you take the flat rate ("safe harbor") Home Office deduction, the costs are included in the flat rate. See **Home Office**.

Service Mark

A service mark is a trademark that applies to a service (trademarks apply to goods). Service marks are amortized (deducted) over a 15-year period. See **Depreciation**.
Expense category: Depreciation (also fill out Form 4562, "Depreciation and Amortization").

Sewer Service

Sewer expenses are part of the Home Office deduction, prorated business versus personal using the same percentage as the home office. If you take the flat rate ("safe harbor") Home Office deduction, the expenses are included in the flat rate. See **Home Office**.

Shipping

Shipping and handling charges are deductible, with some limitations. See **Freight.**
Expense category: Other expenses.

Shipping Supplies

Shipping supplies are deductible unless they are an integral part of the product you are shipping. Then they must be included as part of inventory. See **Inventory**.

Expense category: Supplies (if deductible currently); or Cost-of-goods-sold (if included in inventory).

Shoplifting Losses

Shoplifting losses are deductible as part of cost-of-goods-sold. See **Inventory**.

Showroom

A showroom in your home is part of the Home Office deduction. If you take the flat rate ("safe harbor") Home Office deduction, the expenses are included in the flat rate. See **Home Office**.

The cost of a showroom outside the home is deductible. If you have a rented showroom and a home office, both are deductible if the home office meets the IRS's home office requirements. See **Home Office**.

Expense category: Rent or lease (for rented space); Depreciation (owned building).

Shows

Shows you put on to promote your business are deductible. Food and beverages served are fully deductible. Shows you attend are deductible, although meals you purchase are only 50 percent deductible.

Expense category: Advertising. Other expenses. Meals.

Sick Pay

Employee sick pay is deductible. It is considered regular, taxable wages.

Expense category: Wages.

Self-employed individuals (sole proprietors, partners in partnerships, and members of limited liability companies) cannot deduct their own sick pay, because they are not legally employees of their businesses. See **Draw**, **Paying Yourself**.

Signs

Most signs can, at your option, be deducted the year of purchase or depreciated. Large and expensive outdoor signs, however, are considered land improvements, and are depreciated. See **Business Assets, Depreciation.**

Expense category: Depreciation (also fill out Form 4562, "Depreciation and Amortization").

SIMPLE Plan

"SIMPLE" stands for Savings Incentive Match Plan for Employees, a tax deferred retirement plan. And—I know you're going to be surprised—not all that simple. See **Retirement Plans**.

Expense category: Deducted on Form 1040.

Simplified Employee Pension Plan

A tax-deferred retirement plan. Also known as a SEP or SEP-IRA. See **Retirement Plans**.

Expense category: Deducted on Form 1040.

Smartphones

Smartphones come under the same rules as cell phones. If used 100 percent for business, the phones are 100 percent deductible. If the smartphone is used partly for business, you can deduct the percentage of the cost used for business.

Expense category: Office expenses.

Snacks

I looked this one up. Nowhere in the IRS Code does it mention snacks or say whether snacks are deductible. (*The peanuts are salty.*) The IRS does allow a deduction for expenses that are ordinary and necessary. (*The root beer is cold.*) And everybody knows that snacks are ordinary and necessary. Absolutely. (*We're out of potato chips. Do we get to deduct the mileage driving to the store to get more?*)

Expense category: Office expense.

Social Security Tax

Social Security and Medicare are the two combined payroll taxes deducted from every employee's paycheck and collected from every employer. This pair of taxes is often called FICA (Federal Insurance Contributions Act), or OASDI (Old Age, Survivors and Disability Insurance), or simply Social Security.

The employer's portion of the tax is deductible. That is, the tax that you as an employer pay on behalf of your employees can be deducted on your tax return.

Expense category: Taxes and licenses.

Self-employed individuals: All self-employed people also pay a combined Social Security and Medicare tax; it's called self-employment tax. It is not deductible, though you are allowed a tax deduction for part of it on the 1040 return. See **Self-Employment Tax**.

Software

It's hard to believe how many different tax deduction rules there are for software. The bottom line, however, is that anything that costs $200 or less can be written off when purchased.

Expense category: Office expense.

If you want to explore more options, here they are:

Software bundled with a computer: Software that was packaged with your computer when you bought it is considered part of the cost of the computer. See **Business Assets**.

Leased and subscribed software: Software you rent or lease or subscribe to, including cloud computing, can be written off like any other rental expense.

Expense category: Office expenses.

Purchased "off-the-shelf" software: Regular commercially available software (packaged or as a download) can be written off or depreciated over three years.

Expense category: Office expenses, or Depreciation.

Specialized software: Custom designed and industry-specific software can be written off or depreciated over 15 years. See **Business Assets**.

Software you develop: If you develop software programs, for yourself or for sale to others, you can write off the development costs as current expenses, or depreciate the costs over three years or five years, your option. See **Business Assets, Depreciation**. Software you develop may be eligible for a Research Tax Credit. See **Tax Credits**.

Software Developers

See **Software**.

Some software firms are eligible for the Domestic Production Deduction, also known as the Manufacturer's Deduction. See **Manufacturer's Deduction**.

Solar Power

Solar installations to your home or home office are part of the Home Office deduction. These costs usually have to be depreciated over five years. If the solar installation is for the entire home, the depreciation is prorated business versus personal, using the same percentage as the home office. If you take the flat rate ("safe harbor") Home Office deduction, the solar expenses are included in the flat rate. See **Home Office**.

You may also be eligible for an Energy Tax Credit. See **Tax Credits**.

The truth is that we have such a limited budget, such limited manpower to enforce the income tax laws and collect the revenue, that the only way we can keep them honest and paying their taxes is to keep them afraid.

—Donald Alexander, Former IRS Commissioner

Sponsorships

"Bob's Laundromat All Stars." Sponsor a Little League team, a race car, a rodeo rider, an event, or an individual in a show or competition, and get a full deduction for your business.

Expense category: Advertising.

Spouse

For federal income tax laws, the IRS defines a spouse as anyone who is legally married. The IRS allows spousal deductions for any legally married couple. The IRS does not allow any spousal deductions for couples who are not legally married.

Different states have different definitions of "legally married." Some states recognize common-law marriage, some don't. Some states recognize same-sex marriage, some don't. If your state says you are legally married, the IRS accepts that ruling.

Same sex married couples: If you get legally married in a state that does allow same-sex marriages, but move to another state that does not allow same-sex marriages, the IRS will still allow you to claim all spousal benefits deductions. For the IRS, you do not lose spousal status by moving to another state.

Spouse as employee: You can hire your spouse as an employee of your business, and get a full payroll deduction like you would for any other employee. An employee-spouse is subject to all employee withholding and payroll taxes except for Federal Unemployment (FUTA) taxes. (The FUTA exemption does not apply to corporations.) Putting your spouse on the payroll will also make your spouse and family—including you—eligible for a medical expense deduction. See **Medical Expenses**.

Expense category: Wages.

Spouse's business expenses: Any business expenses your spouse incurs can be deducted only if your spouse is an official employee of your business, or if your spouse is a partner in the business.

Expense category: Varies depending on actual expenses.

Standard Meal Allowance

You are allowed a 50 percent deduction for meals while traveling away from home overnight on business. You can keep track of actual meal expenses, or you may be able to use a per-diem standard meal allowance. IRS Publication 1542, "Per Diem Rates," shows the current per-diem rates for different cities.

If you use per-diem rates, keep in mind that per-diem rates for meals are only 50 percent deductible, because meals are only 50 percent deductible. Whatever per-diem meal rate the IRS lists, you can deduct only half.

Expense category: Meals and entertainment.

Child care providers can, at your option, use the standard meal allowance (even if they are not corporations) or deduct the actual cost of meals.

Standard Mileage Allowance (Rate)

The IRS has a standard mileage allowance deduction (also called a "standard mileage rate") for every business mile driven. This allowance is in lieu of actual vehicle expenses such as gas, oil changes, maintenance, and the cost of the vehicle. This mileage allowance is also in lieu of depreciation and any first-year write-offs (see **Business Assets**). In addition to the mileage allowance, you can also deduct parking (with limitations; see **Parking**), tolls, interest, and property taxes on the vehicle (but not sales tax).

The standard mileage rate is 56¢ per mile. This rate changes, up or down a few cents, every year.

The Standard Mileage Allowance has several restrictions and fine-print rules. See **Vehicles**.

Expense category: Car and truck expenses.

Start-Up Costs

Business expenses incurred before you start operating your business come under a different tax rule than expenses incurred once you are officially open for business. The IRS has two categories of costs associated with starting a business: Organizational Costs and Start-Up Costs.

Organizational Costs apply only to businesses being set up as corporations, and are limited to legal and accounting services and government filing fees to set up the business (though not the cost of selling stock). See **Organizational Costs**.

All other costs of starting a new business (other than costs specifically included in Organizational Costs) come under the Start-Up Costs rules. Up to $5,000 of Start-Up Costs can be deducted the first year of business. Expenses in excess of the $5,000 maximum must be amortized over 15 years. "Amortize" is an accounting term for writing off intangible assets over a period of years. The $5,000 deduction phases out, dollar for dollar, if organizational costs exceed $50,000.

The first-year deduction is optional. You can deduct less than the maximum this year, and spread the balance over 15 years. If your new business hasn't earned much money, and will owe little or no taxes for the current year, by spreading out the start-up costs over 15 years, you will save on future years' taxes.

Start-up costs deductible the year you start your business include costs incurred in previous years, assuming the previous years' costs were not previously deducted. Total deduction for start-up costs (current and previous years combined) is $5,000.

IRS Definition of "Start-Up" Expenses

The IRS says that start-up costs are those that are incurred before "opening day," before the "active trade or business begins" (quotes are from IRS publications). The IRS has often wrangled with taxpayers over which costs are and aren't "start-up," and at what point a new venture is actually "in business." This is an area to discuss with an accountant. I suggest you put off as many expenses as possible until after the business is operating.

One way around some of the start-up expense problems is to start your business as small an operation as possible to meet IRS requirements. Once you have generated a little income, then spend your money on stationery, furniture and equipment, and on accounting and legal advice. Since you are now officially in business, the expenses are deductible as regular business expenses, no longer subject to the start-up rules.

If you do incur start-up expenses but never actually start a business, the expenses may, in some situations, be deductible as a capital loss under the IRS's capital gains and loss rules.

State Taxes

The list of state taxes on businesses is virtually endless. Every state gets to tax its in-state businesses on just about anything the state thinks it can get away with. If your state has a tax on anything, rest assured that you will hear about it. Most state taxes are deductible. Special rules apply to sales tax and income tax.

Sales taxes on purchases you make are deducted as part of the cost of whatever you are buying. Sales taxes you collect from your customers are deducted as a tax expense. See **Sales Tax**.

State income taxes: Generally, only C Corporations can deduct state and local income taxes on their federal returns. Sole proprietorships, partnerships, LLCs, and S corporations do not usually pay income taxes (the owners of these businesses pay the taxes), so no deduction is allowed.

State gross receipts taxes: There is another type of state income tax called a state "gross income" or "gross receipts" tax that, if levied in your state, is deductible for all businesses. This is a tax based on total income before expenses. These taxes are not typically called income taxes, but the IRS often refers to them as income taxes, just to confuse the issue. Do not confuse these "gross" income taxes with regular income taxes: regular income taxes are based on "net" income, that is, income after all business deductions.

Remember that these are IRS rules, for your federal tax return. Your state may or may not allow deductions for state income taxes on your state return.

Expense category: Taxes and licenses.

Stationery

Stationery, envelopes, and other office supplies can be deducted.
Expense category: Office expense.

Stock

Shares of corporate stock (stock certificates) that you purchase are usually not deductible as a business expense.

If you are buying a business—acquiring the corporate stock of a corporation you are buying—you may be able to deduct some of the cost. It is important to talk to your accountant before making such a purchase. A lot of tax money may be at stake, depending on how the purchase is legally structured.

Cost of issuing your own corporate stock may have to be amortized over a period of years. This is another area you should discuss with an accountant.

Inventory: The term "stock" is also used to describe inventory, goods for sale. See **Inventory**.

Livestock on farms may or may not be deductible depending on many factors.

Stolen Property

Stolen depreciable property (business assets that you are depreciating) can be deducted as a casualty loss, but only to the extent of the undepreciated balance. If you deducted the entire asset the first year, you have no deductible loss.

Inventory that is stolen is deducted as part of your cost-of-goods-sold. See **Inventory**.

If stolen property was covered by insurance, you are not allowed a deduction for the loss (since you did not really incur a loss).

Expense category: Depends on what kind of property was stolen. Also fill out Form 4684, "Casualties and Thefts."

Storage Costs and Storage Facilities

A storage area in your home is part of the Home Office deduction. If you take the flat rate ("safe harbor") Home Office deduction, storage area expenses are included in the flat rate. See **Home Office**.

Rent of a storage facility is deductible.

Expense category: Rent or lease, for the rental fees. Other expenses for the incidental costs.

Storage facilities you own can be depreciated or, for some buildings, can be written off the year of purchase. See **Depreciation**.

Store

A store in your home is part of the Home Office deduction. If you take the flat rate ("safe harbor") Home Office deduction, rent or depreciation on the store space is included in the flat rate. See **Home Office**.

The cost of renting or buying a store outside the home is deductible. If you have a rented storefront and a home office, both are deductible if the home office meets the IRS's home office requirements. See **Home Office**.

Expense category: Rent or lease (for rented space); Depreciation (owned building).

Store Fixtures

See **Fixtures**.

Storm Losses

Deductible. See **Casualty Losses**.

Expense category: Depends on kind of property lost, damaged, or destroyed. Also fill out Form 4684, "Casualties and Thefts."

Studio

A studio in your home is part of the Home Office deduction. If you take the flat rate ("safe harbor") Home Office deduction, the expenses are included in the flat rate. See **Home Office**.

The cost of a studio outside the home is deductible. If you have a rented studio and a home office, both are deductible if the home office meets the IRS's home office requirements. See **Home Office**.

Expense category: Rent or lease (for rented space); Depreciation (owned building).

Subcontractors

Subcontractors are usually considered independent contractors, in business for themselves. Their fees are deductible. See **Independent Contractors**.

Expense category: Commissions and fees.

If a subcontractor is constructing or doing major repairs or renovations on a building, the subcontractor's fees may have to be added to the cost of the building, and depreciated. See **Depreciation**.

Expense category: Depreciation. Also fill out Form 4562, "Depreciation and Amortization."

Subscriptions

Subscriptions are deductible.
Expense category: Office expense.

Supplies

Office supplies are deductible. See **Office Supplies**.

Manufacturing supplies are added to the cost of the goods being manufactured, and included in inventory. See **Inventory**.

Supplies that a repair shop sells or uses, and supplies that you use or sell in your trade (such as a plumber or electrician), can be written off when purchased. But if the supplies are replacement parts with significant value, they are considered part of inventory, and cannot be deducted until sold. See **Inventory.**

Shipping supplies are deductible unless they are an integral part of the product you are shipping. Then they must be included as part of inventory. See **Inventory**.

Expense category: Supplies; or (if included in inventory) Cost-of-goods-sold.

Surveys

The cost of conducting surveys is deductible.

Expense category: Legal and professional services.

Surveying costs related to land or buildings may have to be capitalized. See **Buildings, Land**.

SUVs

The deduction for sport utility vehicles is limited. See "Limitations on Vehicles" under **Depreciation**.

Tariffs

Tariffs, customs fees, and duties are deductible. Fees charged by customs brokers and international handlers are deductible. Instead of deducting tariffs immediately, in some cases the fees can be added to the cost of inventory and written off as cost-of-goods-sold. You may want to ask your accountant about this.

Expense category: Commissions and fees. Taxes and licenses.

Tax Credits

Tax credits are special tax incentives created by Congress, to stimulate the economy or to encourage businesses to act in socially or environmentally responsible ways.

Tax credits should not be confused with tax deductions. A tax deduction is an item of expense that reduces your business profit. A tax credit, by comparison, does not reduce your business profit. It reduces your taxes directly, dollar for dollar. For example, a tax deduction of

$100 may save you $30 or $40 in taxes, depending on your tax bracket. A tax credit of $100 will save you a full $100 in taxes, regardless of your tax bracket. Tax credits are a real gold mine.

Some expenses can be taken as both tax credits and tax deductions. You get the deduction to reduce your taxable profit, and you get the tax credit to reduce your taxes!

Tax credits come and go, available one year and not the next. If you fail to take a tax credit you are entitled to, the IRS will not tell you. Last year's business tax credits included:

Alternative Fuels Credit. For using or producing non-fossil fuels and for fuels used off highway and in farming.

Credit for Increased Research Expenses. For some research, experimentation, and development expenses.

Disabled Access Credit. Making your business premises, equipment, and services more accessible to disabled people.

Energy Credit. For solar electric installations.

Electric Vehicle Credit. For purchase of plug-in electric vehicles (not hybrids).

Foreign Income Tax Credit. For taxes paid to another country.

Credit for Employer Paid Social Security Taxes on Employee Cash Tips (FICA Tax Credit). For employers whose employees earn tips.

Small Employer Pension Plan Startup Costs Credit. For starting a pension plan for your employees.

Small Employer Health Insurance Credit. For providing employer-paid health insurance to your employees.

Employer Provided Child Care Credit. For providing child care facilities for your employees.

Low Income Housing Credit. For construction of certain low-income housing.

Rehabilitation Credit. For rehabilitating old buildings and historic structures.

Some tax credits appear on partnership or corporation returns. Other credits are on the 1040 return. The IRS's Publication 334, "Tax Guide for Small Business," lists the current credits.

Taxes

Most taxes other than federal income tax and self-employment tax are deductible. See the listings of specific taxes for more details.

The IRS says that prepaid taxes are not deductible until the year they apply to. Some tax courts disagree. See **Prepayments**.

Expense category: Taxes and licenses.

Sales tax: Sales tax you pay when you purchase goods is added to the cost of the goods, not deducted separately. See **Sales Tax.**

Tax penalties are not deductible. Interest charges on late tax payments are deductible for corporations only. See **Interest Expense**.

Property taxes for a home office come under the Home Office rules. See **Property Taxes**.

Tax Penalties

Tax penalties are not deductible.

What's bad news for some is a bonanza for others. Those tens of billions in costs are going into the pockets of tens of thousands of tax preparers who are organized and love complexity as much as the rest of us hate it.

—Nicholas von Hoffman, columnist

Tax Return Preparation

Fees paid to prepare business tax returns are deductible. For sole proprietors, only the cost of preparing the business part of your 1040 tax return (schedule C or C-EZ and related schedules) is deductible. Ask your accountant to give you a separate bill for the business part of the tax preparation fee.

Expense category: Legal and professional services.

Telephone

Telephones and telephone equipment and devices (answering machines, fax machines, credit card terminals, etc.) can be deducted when purchased or can be depreciated. See **Business Assets**.

Tax deductions for a home telephone land line are limited. You may not deduct the basic monthly rate for the first telephone land line into the home. Expenses beyond the basic rate, such as business-related long distance calls, optional services, Yellow Pages listings, and any special business equipment are deductible. Any additional business lines into the house after the first line are fully deductible if used exclusively for business.

For tax purposes, it does not matter to the IRS how the phone is listed, business or personal. The first land line into your home is not deductible even if it is listed as a business phone, even if it is used 100 percent for business. A second line is fully deductible, regardless of its listing, as long as it is used 100 percent for business.

This rule does NOT apply to cell phones. Cell phones and smart phones used for business are fully deductible. See **Cell Phones**.

Expense category: Office expense.

Temporary Help Agency

Fees paid to an agency or service that provides temporary workers are fully deductible. The workers are not your employees, they are employees of the agency, so this is not a payroll expense.

Expense category: Legal and professional services.

Theft Losses

Theft losses are deductible to the extent they are not covered by insurance. However, there are different rules for different types of losses and different types of businesses. See **Casualty Losses**.

This Book

That's right. The money you paid for this book is 100 percent deductible. In fact, you can deduct twice as much, just by going out and buying a second copy.

Expense category: Office expense.

Tickets

Tickets to events such as sports, music, and theater are considered entertainment. Only 50 percent of the cost can be deducted, and only if there is a valid business reason to buy the tickets. Some tickets to non-profit sporting events are 100 percent deductible.

The deduction must be based on the face value of the ticket. If you paid a scalper or ticket broker $500 for a $100 Rolling Stones ticket, you only get to deduct 50 percent of the $100 face value.

If you buy tickets to give away to a client or prospect, the tickets are no longer entertainment expenses, they are gift expenses. The maximum gift deduction is $25 per recipient per year, and is deductible. See **Business Gifts**.

Buying tickets to entertainment events, like all entertainment expenses, is a red flag to IRS auditors. It might trigger an audit. I often advice tax clients to consider not deducting this expense.

Citations: Parking tickets and speeding tickets and other citations for illegal activities are not deductible.

Raffle tickets are usually considered donations, and only corporations can deduct donations. Senator Ebenezer Scrooge himself must have put through this law.

Expense category: Meals and entertainment (if entertainment). Other expenses (if gift). Charitable contributions (if charitable).

Tips

Tip #1: Don't invest in anything that eats.

Tip #2: Don't tell the IRS auditor that income taxes are unconstitutional.

Tip #3: Tips paid for meal service or entertainment are only 50 percent deductible.

Expense category: Meals and entertainment.

Tip #4: Tips for services other than food are fully deductible.

Expense category: Other expenses.

Restaurant and tavern employers: There is a tax credit for payroll taxes paid on employee tips. See **Tax Credits**.

Tolls

Vehicle tolls are deductible. If you take the standard mileage allowance, tolls are deductible in addition to the mileage allowance.
Expense category: Car and truck expenses.

Tool Allowances/Reimbursements (Employers)

Payments to employees for use of their tools or equipment are considered taxable wages, unless the payments are part of a formal accountable plan. The is a hot-button issue for the IRS. You should talk to an experienced accountant about this.

Tools

Inexpensive tools and tools with a life of a year or less are deductible. More expensive tools can be deducted the year of purchase or depreciated. See **Business Assets, Depreciation**.
Expense category: Supplies (if low cost or short lived); or Depreciation (also fill out Form 4562, "Depreciation and Amortization").

Tractors

Tractors and construction equipment are deducted or depreciated like business assets. See **Business Assets, Depreciation**. They do not come under vehicle rules.
Expense category: Depreciation. Also fill out Form 4562, "Depreciation and Amortization."

Trade

Trade, as in exchange or barter, is a taxable transaction. Goods or services received in trade are deductible at their fair market value. See **Barter**.
Expense category: Depends on what is acquired in trade.

Trade Association

Dues and meetings are deductible.

Expense category: Other expenses.

If part of your dues to a trade or professional association are for political lobbying, that portion of the dues is not deductible.

Trade Dress

Trade dress is a form of trademark. The cost is amortized (deducted) over a 15-year period. See **Depreciation**.

Expense category: Depreciation. Also fill out Form 4562, "Depreciation and Amortization."

Trade Name

Trade names are similar to trademarks. The cost is amortized (deducted) over a 15-year period. See **Depreciation**.

Expense category: Depreciation. Also fill out Form 4562, "Depreciation and Amortization."

Trademark

The cost of obtaining a trademark is amortized (deducted) over a 15-year period. See **Depreciation**.

Expense category: Depreciation. Also fill out Form 4562, "Depreciation and Amortization."

If you acquire rights to a trademark from another business, under a licensing agreement, the payments may need to be capitalized and amortized. There have been different rulings on this deduction. You should discuss this with an experienced accountant.

Expense category: Other expenses.

Trade Show

Admission fees to trade shows are deductible. Travel (with a few exceptions) and lodging are deductible. Meals are 50 percent deductible. See **Travel, Meals**.

Expense category: Other expenses (for the show itself). Travel.

Trailers

If you are living in a trailer, the office space can be deducted if it meets the home office requirements. If the trailer is parked on your home property, being used for business, it is also eligible for the home office deduction. See **Home Office**.

Trailers used in your business (other than as an office) can be deducted or depreciated. See **Business Assets, Depreciation.** Trailers are not considered vehicles, so they do not come under the restrictions the IRS imposes on vehicles.

Training

Training expenses, seminars, videos, manuals, etc. are deductible, within limitations. See **Education Expenses**.

Expense category: Other expenses.

Transit Passes

See **Commuting.**

Transportation

Most transportation expenses are deductible except commuting expenses, home to your regular place of work and back, which are not deductible. See **Travel, Vehicles**.

Expense category: Car and truck expenses; or Travel (for overnight travel); or Other expenses.

Also see **Commuting**.

It has become popular to call the Tax Code, "The IRS Code," suggesting that the IRS is responsible for it. The IRS didn't write it. Congress did. Congress is responsible for the tax mess, Republicans and Democrats alike.

—Kiplinger Tax Letter, Washington, DC

Travel

Local business travel costs, other than commuting, are deductible. While home business owners do not commute to work, there is an important commute rule that you should know. See **Commuting**.

Self-employed individuals are allowed deductions for food and lodging and miscellaneous expenses only if you are away from home overnight. Home is defined as your place of business, not where you live. See **Food, Lodging**.

Self-employed itinerant workers, traveling contractors, and salespeople who are continually on the road are often denied travel deductions, the IRS claiming that the road is home, so nothing allowed. If you are working away from home for over one year, the IRS automatically considers the road to be home, and disallows travel expenses.

Business Trips Within the U.S. A business trip within the United States that is 100 percent business is 100 percent deductible. That includes round trip travel, lodging, transportation, and incidental expenses such as telephone, fax, laundry, etc. Two exceptions: Meals and entertainment are only 50 percent deductible. Deductions for travel on luxury boats or cruise ships have some limitations (check with the IRS).

Business Trips Outside the U.S. A business trip outside the United States may be 100 percent deductible (with the exceptions of meals, entertainment, and luxury water travel). But if you attend overseas conventions, seminars, or meetings, a deduction is allowed only if the meeting is directly related to your business and if, in the IRS's opinion, there is a valid business reason for holding the meeting overseas. (Some countries are exempt from this restriction; check with the IRS.)

Business and Vacation Combined. What about a trip that is part business and part vacation? You may be able to deduct some of it, and you may be able to deduct all of it, if you carefully follow the rules.

If the reason for your trip is primarily personal (more than half the days are for vacation), none of the traveling expenses to and from your destination are deductible. Only expenses directly related to your business can be deducted.

If your trip is primarily for business (more than half the days are for business) and it is within the United States, the cost of the round-trip travel is fully deductible even if some of the trip is for pleasure. So you can tack a short vacation onto a business trip, and the only costs that aren't deductible are the non-business expenses, such as the extra days' lodging and meals and entertainment.

If you have a business trip that overlaps a weekend, requiring you to be there Friday and the following Monday, lucky you: you can write off the weekend as well, as a business expense, even though all you did was sit on the beach and dance in the clubs (as long as it is less expensive to stay the weekend than to go home Friday and come back Monday morning).

If you travel outside the U.S., more stringent rules apply. If the trip is no more than one week or the time spent for pleasure is less than 25 percent, the same basic rules apply as a trip within the U.S. But if the trip is more than a week, or if the vacation days are 25 percent or more of the trip, you allocate travel expenses between the business and the personal portion of your trip.

When counting business versus vacation days, a "business day" does not require you to do business all day. Any day you put in at least four hours of work is considered a business day. Any day your presence is required, for any amount of time, is considered a business day. And travel days count as business days.

Deductible Expenses

Travel expenses typically include cost of transportation for you and your luggage to and from your destination; lodging and 50 percent of the cost of meals including tips (must not be "lavish or extravagant"); cost of transportation while away from home (taxi fares, auto rentals, etc.); entertainment, subject to the 50 percent limit; incidental expenses such as phone and fax; personal services (laundry, barbering, etc.).

Keeping Track of Expenses

For meals, lodging and incidental expenses, you can keep a record of actual expenses or, for some businesses, you can use a standard "per-diem" rate set by the IRS—so much per day. See **Per Diem** and **Standard Meal Allowance** for more information.

Spouse, Family, Friend, Etc.

Travel expenses are not deductible for your spouse, dependent, friend, or anyone else, unless he or she is an employee or co-owner of the business, and there is a bona fide business purpose for accompanying you. This is a fairly new law. Husbands and wives used to be able to accompany their wives and husbands. This law was pushed through by a congressman who travels all over the world on a luxury military jet at taxpayer expense.

You can still deduct what it would cost you to travel alone. When deducting lodging, for example, you can write off the single-occupant rate at the hotel, which is often the same or slightly less than a double-occupant or family rate you will actually pay.

IRS Red Flag Audit Warning: The IRS does not like business trips. As you can tell from the generous way the law is written, it's a bit too easy to write off a business trip that is really a disguised vacation. The IRS knows this all too well, and they are forever suspicious of business travel expenses, particularly sole proprietorships where the owner is accountable to no one else: you feel like taking a business trip (and you can afford it), you take it. The IRS wants to be sure it's not a vacation in disguise. You want to be sure you can prove, if audited, that the trip wasn't a vacation. A log of daily activities and business contacts is not required by law, but it may help convince a skeptical IRS auditor that your trip to the Bahamas or to New Orleans really was for business. Take photographs of businesses you visited, or goods you want to carry.

For more information see IRS Publication 463, "Travel, Entertainment, and Gift Expenses." For per-diem rates and details, see IRS Publication 1542, "Per Diem Rates."

Expense category: Travel.

Employers can reimburse employees for travel expenses and get a deduction, but you must be careful to follow the rules. See **Reimbursements**.

Travel agents: Travel agents often claim that they need to travel in order to be able to better advise their clients, that such travel expenses are "ordinary" and "necessary" expenses of their business and are therefore fully deductible. The IRS does not always agree. In audits, the IRS sometimes allows those deductions, and sometimes disallows the deductions. This is an area that invites audits, especially if the travel expenses are significant compared to the income generated from the business.

Trips, Business

Most business trips are deductible. See **Travel.**
Expense category: Travel.

Trucks

Trucks used for business can be deducted or depreciated like other vehicles. Vehicles have special limitations. See **Vehicles.**

Expense category: The category "Car and truck expenses" is for all vehicle expenses except the cost of the vehicle itself, which is deducted or depreciated under "Depreciation" (also fill out Form 4562, "Depreciation and Amortization").

Tuition

Some tuition is deductible. See **Education Expenses**.

Uncashed Checks

Are uncashed checks deductible? An uncashed check was not really paid, was it? So it really isn't deductible. But most people take the deduction anyway and figure the check will get cashed sooner or later. A check written and mailed (or delivered) by December 31 can be written off the year it was written, even though it was not cashed until the new year.

If the check is never cashed (lost, voided, returned, stop payment), the expense, assuming you took the deduction when you wrote the check, should be reversed out.

Uncollectible Accounts

Uncollectible accounts are deductible as bad debts, but only if they were included in your income when you made the sale. Businesses using the cash method of accounting (recording income when the money comes in, not when the sale was made) cannot take a deduction for uncollectible accounts, because the income was not recorded in the first place. See **Bad Debts.**

Expense category: Bad debts.

Your own time: Unless you are an employee of your own corporation, you are not allowed a tax deduction for your own time. If you are unable to collect from a client for your time billed to the client, you cannot take a deduction for this lost income. See **Paying Yourself**.

"Under the Table" Payments

Did you actually look this item up, or just stumble upon it?

This interesting term, "under the table," means that a payment has been made, secretly, in cash, and no record is made of the payment. Under the table payments are sometimes made (so I'm told) to workers who are not officially on the payroll, to avoid payroll taxes and workers' compensation insurance premiums, which is illegal and very risky and not a good idea at all.

But is an under the table payment deductible? If the payment was illegal, no deduction is allowed. If the secret payment was for some other reason and was legal (stranger things have happened in the business world), it is deductible. But if you didn't record it, you might have a difficult time proving it was made—and explaining why it was made—to an IRS auditor.

The term "off the books" means the same thing as "under the table."

Expense category: Depends on what the expense was for.

Unemployment Insurance

Employers pay state and federal unemployment insurance (also called unemployment taxes) for their employees. This tax is deductible.

Sole proprietors, partners in partnerships, and members (owners) of limited liability companies are not subject to federal unemployment insurance. If you are required to pay state unemployment insurance, it is deductible.

Expense category: Insurance.

Unemployment Taxes

This is the same as **Unemployment Insurance** (see above). Employer's unemployment taxes are deductible.

Expense category: Taxes and licenses.

Uniforms

Uniforms used exclusively for work are deductible. This includes costumes and protective gear. Cost of cleaning is deductible.

Clothing with your company's logo or advertising is considered a uniform, and therefore deductible.

Expense category: Supplies.

Unions

Dues and meetings are deductible.

Expense category: Other expenses.

If part of your union dues are for political lobbying, that portion of the dues is not deductible.

Unsalable Goods

Unsalable goods can be deducted as part of cost-of-goods-sold. See **Inventory**.

Expense category: Cost-of-goods-sold.

Use Tax

Businesses are not usually required to collect sales tax on out-of-state sales. But in most states, the buyer is supposed to pay sales tax on mail-order and Internet purchases from out-of-state vendors—not to the seller, but directly to the state where you, the buyer, reside (unless the purchases are for resale).

No, I'm not kidding. When you buy a computer or office supplies from an out-of-state company, your own state wants you to pay sales tax on the purchase. It is called a use tax.

On your sales tax return, you will find a line where you calculate the use tax you owe, and pay it along with the sales tax you collected from your customers.

Any inventory or parts purchased tax-free but later used for a purpose other than resale, such as personal use, are also subject to the use tax.

This use tax is deductible. Normally, sales tax (which the use tax really is) is added to the cost of the goods. But since the use tax is paid after the fact, most businesses deduct it as another business tax.

There is a federal excise tax on truckers called a Highway Use Tax. This is a completely different tax than the use tax described above. It also is deductible.

Expense category: Taxes and licenses.

Utilities

Utility expenses are part of the Home Office deduction. Costs for the entire home are prorated business versus personal using the same percentage as the home office. Utility expenses just for the office are fully deductible. If you take the flat rate ("safe harbor") Home Office deduction, utility expenses are included in the flat rate. See **Home Office**.

Renewable resources: You may be eligible for a tax credit if you produce or use electricity from alternative sources. See **Tax Credits**.

People make a mistake when they pay their legislators good salaries, expect them to work full time, and then complain about all the government intervention in their lives. The nature of legislators is to legislate. They work full time introducing new bills that create more agencies, bureaus, commissions and regulatory functions of government.

—H. R. Richardson, Former California Senator

Vacation

Can you write off part of your vacation as a business expense? Yes, if it is combined with a legitimate business trip and if you follow the rules. See **Travel.**

Expense category: Travel.

Vacation Pay (Employers)

An employer can deduct vacation pay for employees. The pay is treated as regular taxable wages.

Expense category: Wages.

Vandalism

Deductible to the extent not covered by insurance.

Expense category: Depends on what kind of property was vandalized, and what costs are incurred.

Vans

Vans, busses, and transporters used for business can be deducted or depreciated like other vehicles. Vehicles have special limitations. See **Vehicles**.

Expense category: The category "Car and truck expenses" is for all vehicle expenses except the cost of the vehicle itself, which is deducted or depreciated under "Depreciation" (also fill out Form 4562, "Depreciation and Amortization").

Vehicles

All expenses of operating a vehicle for business are deductible except regular commuting expenses, which the IRS considers personal and not deductible. (Leased automobiles have certain limitations; see below.) There are two ways of figuring vehicle expenses.

Method 1: You can keep itemized records of all your vehicle expenses. These include gasoline, oil, lubrication, maintenance, repairs, insurance, parking, tolls, garage rents, license and registration fees, even auto club dues. Cost of major repairs such as an engine overhaul may be deducted the year of purchase (with limitations) or depreciated over several years. The purchase price of the vehicle may or may not be deducted the year of purchase, or may have to be depreciated, depending on the type of vehicle and the cost of the vehicle. See "Limitations on vehicles" under **Depreciation**.

Keeping itemized records of all your vehicle expenses, and dealing with the depreciation limitations, is tedious work. The IRS realizes this also. In one of their rare helpful moods they have come up with Method Two, an optional Standard Mileage Allowance (Standard Mileage Rate):

Method 2: Instead of recording each fill up and every oil change, you may take a standard flat rate for every business mile driven (again, not including the commute). The standard mileage rate is 56¢ per mile. This rate changes, up or down a few cents, every year.

This mileage allowance is in lieu of depreciation or First-Year Write-Off, and all vehicle expenses except parking (with limitations; see **Parking**), tolls, interest, and state and local taxes, which are deductible in addition to the mileage allowance (sales tax on the vehicle is not deductible).

Business vs. personal use: Vehicle expenses are prorated between personal use (not deductible) and business use (fully deductible). The most common method of proration is based on the miles driven. For example, if you drove 10,000 miles last year of which 2,500 miles was for business, 25 percent of all your vehicle expenses are deductible, and 25 percent of the cost of your vehicle can be deducted or depreciated.

Keeping records: If you use your personal vehicle for business, the IRS requires that you keep a daily log of business miles driven, including time of day, destination, and business purpose. If you are audited and you don't have a daily logbook, or if you only have estimates or summaries, the IRS will disallow your deduction.

Some fine print: You may not use the Standard Mileage Allowance if you use the vehicle for hire such as a taxi, or if your business operates more than four vehicles at a time. Business vehicles that do not qualify for the Standard Mileage Allowance may still use Method 1, itemizing expenses.

If you use the Standard Mileage Allowance, when you sell the vehicle you must reduce the "cost basis" of the vehicle (for figuring profit or loss when you sell the vehicle) by 22¢ per mile for every business mile driven, all years combined.

The method you choose the first year you use your vehicle for business determines what methods you can use in future years (for that vehicle). If you use Method 1 (itemizing) the first year, you must stay with that method as long as you use that vehicle. If you use Method 2 (the Standard Mileage Allowance) the first year, you can switch back and forth if you want, itemizing some years and using the mileage allowance other years. If you do switch from the mileage allowance to itemizing, you must use straight line depreciation. (Yes, some legislator actually dreamed up this rule.)

Depreciation and first-year-write-off on a vehicle are limited if the vehicle costs over a certain amount.

You should check with your accountant to find out the most advantageous way to write off your vehicle.

IRS Red Flag Audit Warning: People who claim 100 percent business use of a vehicle increase their audit chances. IRS agents know that it's rare for an individual to actually use a vehicle 100 percent for business, especially if no other vehicle is available for personal use.

Expense category: "Car and truck expenses" is for all vehicle expenses except the cost of the vehicle itself, which is deducted or depreciated under "Depreciation" (also fill out Form 4562, "Depreciation and Amortization").

Trade ins: If you trade in a business vehicle on another business vehicle, the undepreciated balance of the old vehicle has to be figured in the cost basis of the new vehicle, for figuring depreciation. It may be to your advantage to sell the old vehicle instead of trading it in. Ask your accountant about this.

Leasing and rentals: Automobile leases, if 30 days or longer, are not 100 percent deductible. The IRS has a table, called "Inclusion Amounts for Cars," that shows how much of an auto lease can and cannot be deducted. See IRS Publication 463 for the table. This rule does not apply to trucks, vans, or heavy sport utility vehicles, which are fully deductible.

Electric Vehicles: You may be eligible for a tax credit when you purchase a plug-in electric vehicle (not a hybrid). See **Tax Credits**.

Company cars: Personal (non-business) use of company-owned vehicles by an employee is considered taxable wages to the employee, subject to all payroll taxes.

For more information, see IRS Publication 917, "Business Use of a Car" and IRS Publication 463, "Travel, Entertainment, Gift and Car Expenses."

Video and Film Producers

Some video and film producers are eligible for the Domestic Production Deduction, also known as the Manufacturer's Deduction. See **Manufacturer's Deduction**.

Voided Checks

It must be pretty obvious that you do not get a deduction for a voided check you wrote and then tore up. If you don't void the check immediately, and you've already taken a deduction for it, reverse the deduction out of your ledgers. Also see **Bounced Checks**.

Wages

Employee wages are deductible. See **Payroll**.
Expense category: Wages.
If your business is not a corporation, your own wages—that is, the wages you pay yourself if you pay yourself a wage—are not a deductible business expense. See **Draw, Paying Yourself**.

Warehouse

The cost of warehouse space in your home is part of the Home Office deduction. If you take the flat rate ("safe harbor") Home Office deduction, costs related to the space are included in the flat rate. See **Home Office**.
The cost of renting a warehouse is deductible. The cost of a building (or part of a building) you own can be depreciated. See **Buildings**. If you have a rented warehouse and a home office, both are deductible if the home office meets the IRS's home office requirements. See **Home Office**.
Expense category: Rent or lease (for rented space); Depreciation (owned building).

Warranties

Extended warranties, which you pay extra for, are deductible if they do not extend beyond 12 months. See **Prepayments**.
Expense category: Repairs and maintenance.

Watchdog

There is no IRS ruling or code section spelling out what kind of deduction is allowed for a home-business watchdog. I suggest that businesses deduct this expense as part of the Home Office, just like utilities and maintenance. See **Home Office**.

Water

You can deduct a percentage of your home utilities if you are allowed a home office deduction. See **Home Office**.

Website

The cost of designing, setting up, and maintaining a website is deductible. If the initial design cost is significant, it may have to be amortized (depreciated) over three years. See **Depreciation**.

Hosting fees and costs of maintaining a website are deductible. Domain name registration and fees are deductible.

The cost of Internet access is fully deductible if used only for business. If used partly for non-business, you prorate the cost and deduct only the business portion.

Expense category: Advertising (web page); Depreciation (expensive website); Office expense (access, hosting, etc.).

You must market your product and your company as though you are not working out of your attic or basement. Customers, like banks, tend to trust static investments like buildings and furniture rather than dynamic ones like product development and marketing.

—David W. Jensen, owner, Lupine Dog Accessories

Wife on Payroll

See **Spouse**.

Work Clothes

Deductible only if unsuitable for street wear, or if it is a uniform; see **Uniforms**.

Clothing with your company's logo or advertising is fully deductible, even though the clothing may be suitable for street wear.

Cost of cleaning work clothes is deductible.

Expense category: Supplies, or Advertising.

Workers' Compensation Insurance

Workers' compensation insurance an employer pays to cover employees is deductible.

Workers' compensation insurance you pay for yourself is deductible only if your state requires you to have workers' comp insurance on yourself. If the coverage is voluntary, the premiums are not deductible (except for corporations).

Expense category: Insurance.

Work in Process

Work in process (also called work in progress) is a manufacturing term for a product that is partially completed. Work in process is part of your inventory and cannot be deducted until sold. See **Inventory**.

Expense category: Cost-of-goods-sold.

Workshop

The cost of a workshop in your home is part of the Home Office deduction. If you take the flat rate ("safe harbor") Home Office deduction, expenses related to the workshop space are included in the flat rate. See **Home Office**.

The cost of renting a workshop is deductible. The cost of a building (or part of a building) you own can be depreciated. See **Buildings**. If you have a rented workshop and a home office, both are deductible if the home office meets the IRS's home office requirements. See **Home Office**.

Expense category: Rent or lease (for rented space); Depreciation (owned building).

Worthless Goods

Worthless inventory can be written off as part of cost-of-goods-sold. See **Inventory**.

Worthless business assets that have already been fully deducted cannot be deducted a second time. If the assets are being depreciated, the remaining undepreciated balance can be deducted. For example, let's say you bought a piece of equipment a few years ago for $4,000, and you've already taken $2,500 depreciation on it. It dies and isn't worth fixing. Since you've already deducted $2,500, you can only deduct $1,500, which is the undepreciated balance.

Expense category: Depreciation. Also fill out Form 4562, "Depreciation and Amortization."

Yellow Pages

Yellow Pages listings and advertising are deductible.
Expense category: Advertising.

Zoning

Zoning costs for land rezoning (such as residential to commercial) or for building construction are added to the cost of the home. See **Buildings**.

Zoning costs for any other business purposes, including permits, filings, hearings, appeals, petitions, etc. are deductible.
Expense category: Taxes and licenses.

About the Author

Bernard B. Kamoroff is a certified public accountant with more than thirty years' experience, specializing in small business.

Mr. Kamoroff has worked directly with hundreds of businesses and has been a guest speaker at business, professional, and trade association meetings and conventions.

He has given business workshops and seminars for the University of California, American River College, Mendocino College, Open Exchange, Learning Annex, American Booksellers Association, Marketing Boot Camp, and San Francisco Business Renaissance.

Mr. Kamoroff is the author of five business guidebooks, including *Small Time Operator: How to Start Your Own Business, Keep Your Books, Pay Your Taxes, and Stay Out of Trouble*, now in its thirteenth edition.

In addition to helping other businesses, Mr. Kamoroff has started and successfully operated three of his own small businesses.

Bernard Kamoroff lives in Mendocino County, California. If you have any questions, suggestions, or comments about *Write It Off! Deduct It!*, please send them to the author, c/o Bell Springs Publishing, Box 1240, Willits, CA 95490. Or e-mail kamoroff@bellsprings.com. Also be sure to visit the author's website at http://www.bellsprings.com.